Gabriele Esposito

Armies Across History no. 3

South American Armies 1825–1865
Organization, uniforms and weapons

Table of contents

Preface 3
Introduction 5
Military conflicts in the River Plate region, 1810–1865 7
Military conflicts in the Andean and Caribbean regions, 1825–1865 12
The Brazilian Army 15
The Argentine Army 44
The Uruguayan Army 71
The Paraguayan Army 97
The Peruvian Army 104
The Chilean Army 117
The Bolivian Army 124
The Colombian Army 130
The Venezuelan Army 141
The Ecuadorian Army 146
Select Bibliography 152

Published in Poland in 2023
by STRATUS sp.j.
ul. Żeromskiego 6A,
27-600 Sandomierz, Poland

as
MMPBooks,
3 Gloucester Close,
Petersfield
Hampshire GU32 3AX, UK
e-mail: office@mmpbooks.biz
© 2023 MMPBooks.
http://www.mmpbooks.biz

All rights reserved. Apart from any fair dealing for the purpose of private study, research, criticism or review, as permitted under the Copyright, Design and Patents Act, 1988, no part of this publication may be reproduced, stored in a retrieval system, or transmitted in any form or by any means, electronic, electrical, chemical, mechanical, optical, photocopying, recording or otherwise, without prior written permission. All enquiries should be addressed to the publisher.

ISBN
978-83-66549-96-8

Editor in chief
Roger Wallsgrove

Editorial Team
Bartłomiej Belcarz
Robert Pęczkowski
Arthur Juszczak

Cover
Artur Juszczak

DTP:
Stratus sp. j.

PRINTED IN POLAND

About the author

Gabriele Esposito is a military historian who works as a freelance author and researcher for some of many publishing houses in the military history sector. In particular, he is an expert specializing in uniformology. His interests and expertise range from ancient civilizations to modern post-colonial conflicts. During recent years he has conducted and published much research on the military history of Latin American countries, with special attention on the War of the Triple Alliance and the War of the Pacific. He is among the leading experts on the military history of the Italian Wars of Unification and the Spanish Carlist Wars. His books and essays are published on a regular basis by Osprey Publishing, Pen & Sword, Winged Hussar Publishing and Libreria Editrice Goriziana. He is also the author of numerous military history articles appearing in specialized magazines like *Ancient Warfare Magazine*, *Medieval Warfare Magazine*, *The Armourer*, *History of War*, *Guerres et Histoire*, *Focus Storia* and *Focus Storia Wars*.

Preface

The present book would have been impossible without the support of some very special friends, who all gave their precious contribution to the efforts that led to the creation of this work. First of all, I want to express my deep gratitude to my old friend Giuseppe Martini who supplied me all the rare primary sources from which the info contained in this work was taken and who assembled most of the colour pictures printed in the present book. Giuseppe is a loyal friend and one of the world's greatest experts of military history, who has conducted researches on the armies of South America for the past fifteen years. A very special thanks goes to Patricio Greve Moller, one of the greatest South American military historians of the present times, for having painted 68 of the magnificent uniforms reproduced in this book. Patricio is a brilliant historian but also a talented illustrator, whose detailed and colourful art brought back to life many South American uniforms that had never been reconstructed before in a graphic way. For more details about Patricio's many publications and activities, it is possible to visit his fantastic website dedicated to military history: https://militariabloghistoricomilitar.blogspot.com/. The author also wants to express his personal gratitude to Eduardo Espinosa Mora, for providing some of the colour plates dedicated to the uniforms of Ecuador. Eduardo is the greatest military historian of Ecuador and has worked very hard during recent years in order to produce some excellent military history publications in his country. A big thanks is also due to my father, the "maestro" Benedetto Esposito, for creating the magnificent colour plates dedicated to the Gran Colombian Army. His natural talent and vivid style always give something special to his excellent works of art. Finally, the author wants to express his deep gratitude to the Anne S.K. Brown Military Collection for making available on its fantastic website (https://repository.library.brown.edu/studio/collections/bdr:224400/) the astonishing works of art of some legendary military artists like Louis de Beaufort and Francisco Ferrer Llull.

Introduction

When South America's Wars of Independence ended in 1825, the geographical map of that part of the world was completely different from the actual one. Several new states, in fact, had emerged and were still building their national identity at the expense of the bordering countries. In the northern part of the continent there was the large confederation known as Gran Colombia, created by Simón Bolívar, which had been the main driving force behind the liberation of the northern half of South America from Spanish colonial rule. In the western part of the continent there was Peru, a young nation with strong expansionist ambitions. Present-day Bolivia was still occupied by Gran Colombian troops, Chile was fully independent but quite marginal from a political point of view. The immense Empire of Brazil dominated over the eastern portion of South America, Paraguay was the poorest and most isolated of the new republics. In the River Plate region there was the Argentine Republic, which had been the main driving force behind the liberation of the southern half of South America from the Spaniards. Very soon the political history of independent South America started to be characterized by the peculiar phenomenon known as "*caudillismo*", i.e. the emergence of some military leaders – national or local – who had great personal ambitions and who could count on the support of some military forces to impose their will.

The young countries of the continent were dominated by landowners who were extremely rich and who wanted to pursue their own interests without being "disturbed" too much by the new governments that had emerged in their home territories. The general organization of the economy and society had not yet changed a lot compared with that of the days of the Spanish/Portuguese rule, since the landowners wanted to continue benefiting from their traditional privileges. In each country, however, there was a growing middle class that wanted to limit the power of these *Caudillos* by adopting liberal political measures and by organizing social life in a democratic way. As a result of this situation, in each of the South American nations two main political entities emerged, a conservative party that protected the interests of the landowners and a liberal party that was the voice of the middle class. The great political differences existing between these opposing groups led to the outbreak of many civil wars in each of South America's states and were one of the main reasons behind the chronic instability of that part of the world. From 1825, in fact, all the countries of the continent started to experience military coups and internal disturbances that were – in most cases – extremely violent. The young military forces of each of the new states played a prominent role in this political process, which lasted for most of the 19th century. Some countries of South America – like Colombia or Venezuela – spent their first eight decades of life being ravaged by civil wars and thus could develop their own institutions only very slowly. Other nations, like Chile, enjoyed more internal stability and thus could develop themselves in an effective way.

Civil conflicts were not the only wars taking place in South America, of course; as anticipated above, in fact, the process of nation-building in that area of the world was strongly linked to military expansionism. From 1825, as soon as the Spanish and Portuguese troops left the area, new conflicts broke out between the young states of the continent. In the northern half of the latter Peru – liberated jointly by Argentina and Gran Colombia – wanted to annex Bolivia as well as the southern territories of Gran Colombia. The latter was a confederation of four states: Colombia, Venezuela, Ecuador and Panama. Since the border dividing Peru from Ecuador was not well defined and since Bolivia had always been united with Peru during the colonial period, the Peruvians were eager to defeat their liberator Bolívar in order to expand their country. As a result, in 1828–1829, Gran Colombia and Peru fought against each other in a bloody conflict that ended with a Gran Colombian victory on land and with a Peruvian victory at sea. Following the end of the hostilities the Gran Colombian troops had to evacuate Bolivia and thus the latter became a fully independent nation. The territory of Ecuador, however, remained intact under Gran Colombian control. The confederation of states created by Bolívar had many internal problems and was not going to last for long. Each of the nations that made up Gran Colombia, in fact, was under the control of *Caudillos* who wanted to become independent from the confederation as soon as possible.

In 1830, a few weeks before Bolívar's death, Venezuela and Ecuador seceded from Gran Colombia and became autonomous nations. Colombia – at that time still known as "*Nueva Grenada*" – retained control only of Panama. The three nations emerging from the collapse of Gran Colombia were extremely weak from their foundation and were devastated by bloody civil wars until the beginning of the 20th century. Their governments were never true "democratic" ones and their military forces struggled for long time in order to look – at least partially – as professional institutions. In Colombia, Venezuela and Ecuador the phenomenon of "*caudillismo*" corresponded to anarchy. Every year, in fact, there were coups mounted by ambitious landowners or military commanders, which often degenerated into full-scale civil conflicts. Peru and Bolivia, instead, enjoyed some periods of relative internal stability between one internal war and another. During 1836–1839 the two states were united into a short-lived confederation that was soon destroyed by Chile (receiving some marginal assistance from Argentina). In 1841 the Peruvians tried to invade Bolivia, but were utterly defeated and finally had to accept that the Bolivians were going to remain independent.

Brazil was with no doubts the most important political, economic and military power of South America. The Brazilian territory was immense if compared to that of the young

Spanish-speaking republics bordering it and had enormous natural resources. The process that led to the independence of Brazil was much simpler if compared to the "Wars of Liberation" fought by the former Spanish colonies. First of all, the various regions of South America that were dominated by the Portuguese already had all the basic features of a "national state" well before 1825. Their economies were well integrated and their administration was quite centralized. As a result, it was quite natural for them to remain together as a single and vast new country after gaining autonomy. The young Brazilian state became independent after some minor fighting, which was a sort of "civil war" between those Portuguese troops (the majority) who wanted to make Brazil autonomous from the motherland and the few Portuguese troops who were opposed to the separation from Portugal. In the end the former prevailed quite rapidly and Brazil became independent under the rule of Pedro I (son and heir to the throne of the King of Portugal). The whole process was a sort of "family affair", which did not change in a significant way the political situation existing in Brazil. Due to their great expanse, the Brazilian territories were officially organized as the "Empire of Brazil" and thus remained as the only monarchy existing in South America until 1889. The imperial regime was favourable to the great landowners of the country and thus had a quite conservative political attitude. In time, however, the Brazilian liberals became increasingly stronger and this led to the outbreak of some civil wars. The latter saw the temporary secession of some territories, like the southernmost Brazilian state of Rio Grande do Sul that struggled for its autonomy during the turbulent years 1835–1845. By 1850, however, the whole territory of Brazil was fully pacified under the rule of the imperial government.

In the River Plate, Argentina was the dominant regional power and co-existed with the two minor republics of Paraguay and Uruguay (the latter were for a long time considered as part of their national territory by the Argentines, since they had been included into the Spanish Viceroyalty of the River Plate together with Argentina). The former had become independent in 1811, after having repulsed an Argentine invasion and after having expelled the few Spanish authorities settled on Paraguayan territory. From 1811 Paraguay was placed under the iron rule of strong dictators and thus did not experience significant internal disturbances. The country started its life as the most underdeveloped nation of South America (being landlocked and located between two "giants" like Brazil and Argentina), but its economy soon started to benefit from internal stability and international isolation.

The struggle for independence in Uruguay began in 1811, when José Gervasio Artigas freed most of the country from the Spaniards with the objective of making the "*Banda Oriental*" or "Eastern Bank" of the River Plate part of the new Argentine state (created in 1810). In 1814 the joint Argentine-Uruguayan military forces conquered Montevideo, the most important city of the Eastern Bank and the last Spanish stronghold of the latter region, after a long siege. Two years later, however, the Brazilians took advantage of the political differences existing between Artigas and the main Argentine leaders by invading Uruguay. The latter was added to Portuguese Brazil as the Cisplatine Province, following Argentina's refusal to fight for the freedom of the Eastern Bank. This was something natural from a historical point of view, since the Spaniards and the Portuguese had fought several wars for possession of the Uruguayan territory during the 18th century.

In the present book we will provide a detailed description of the organization, uniforms and weapons of the ten South American armies during the so-called "Age of *Caudillos*" (1825–1865), Brazilian, Argentine, Uruguayan, Paraguayan, Peruvian, Chilean, Bolivian, Colombian, Ecuadorian and Venezuelan. From a historical point of view, the "Age of *Caudillos*" began as soon as the Spaniards and the Portuguese left South America in 1825. For the River Plate countries it ended in 1865, with the outbreak of the greatest military conflict in the history of South America (the "Paraguayan War", which ended in 1870). The latter, in fact, obliged Brazil and Argentina to complete their process of nation-building in a definitive way and transformed the armies of the River Plate's states into fully-professional fighting forces. After 1870, at least in countries like Brazil and Argentina, there was no more space for the personal political ambitions of the *Caudillos*.

In the following pages we will describe the general evolution of the ten armies taken into account by describing, in a general way, their histories. As a result, we will also provide an overview of the major conflicts that were fought in South America during the crucial years 1825–1870. When dealing with the military history of the South American countries it is important to remember that local civil wars were quite often linked to inter-state conflicts. This was particularly true for Argentina and Uruguay, since the political parties of the countries formed trans-national alliances between themselves that lasted for many decades. As will emerge from the pages of the present work, the military history of South America during the early 19th century was incredibly eventful. As a result, it deserves more coverage in English and the present book is an important step in this direction. The ten armies analysed in the text all had their own peculiar organization, uniforms and weapons, that were sometimes quite different from those of the contemporary European armies. These have never been studied before in a systematic way due to a series of prejudices that have always affected the military reputation of the South American nations. The present book is designed to work as an illustrated "military history atlas" for the period 1825–1865, providing data and visual materials that have never been published before in Europe. The main objective is that of filling an important gap in the coverage of the 19th century's military history.

Military conflicts in the River Plate region, 1810–1865

- **1810–1811:** In May 1810 Argentina proclaims her autonomy from Spain by organizing an autonomous revolutionary government, though formal independence, however, is not yet proclaimed. The other two countries making up the Spanish "Viceroyalty of the River Plate" (Uruguay and Paraguay) remain loyal to the Spanish authorities. In the early weeks of 1811 the Argentines sent an army commanded by the experienced Manuel Belgrano to Paraguay, with the objective of annexing the latter. The Argentine troops were soundly defeated by the Paraguayan militias at the Battles of Paraguarí (19 January 1811) and Tacuarí (9 March 1811). The Paraguayans were able to repulse the Argentine invasion without receiving any support from the Spanish colonial authorities and thus decided to expel the latter from their home territory. On 14 May 1811 Paraguay proclaimed its independence and a few weeks later, on 12 October, the country signed a treaty with Argentina, according to which Paraguay would become part of a larger confederation of autonomous states that would be formed in the River Plate (something that never materialized). Meanwhile, in Uruguay the local patriots start their uprising against Spain on 28 February 1811. On 18 May of the same year the leader of the Uruguayan insurgents, the brilliant military commander José Gervasio Artigas, obtained a clear victory over the Spaniards at the Battle of Las Piedras. With Argentine support the Uruguayans start besieging the last Spanish stronghold of Montevideo, but the military intervention of Portuguese Brazil in favour of the Spaniards temporarily suspended the siege.
- **1812–1814:** Argentina fights against the Spaniards coming from Bolivia on her north-western borders and resumed the besieging operations of Montevideo. The Argentines were strongly supported by Artigas, who wanted to unify Uruguay with Argentina but without renouncing the autonomy of his country. Some Argentine leaders were favourable to the idea of creating a confederation of provinces, comprising also Uruguay, while others simply wanted to annex the latter nation to their country. In 1814 hostilities commenced between Artigas' troops and the Argentine forces operating in Uruguay. Several provinces of north-eastern Argentina, ruled by autonomous *Caudillos*, decided to side with the Uruguayan leader and support his federalist plans. On 22 February 1814 the Argentines were defeated by Artigas at the Battle of El Espinillo. Later, on 23 May of the same year, Montevideo was conquered by the Argentines and the last Spanish troops were expelled from the River Plate. Meanwhile, in Paraguay, José Gaspar Rodríguez de Francia assumed dictatorial powers.
- **1815–1820:** Argentina and Uruguay were ravaged by their first major civil war, fought between two emerging political parties. On one side there were the "*Unitarios*", who want to organize the Argentine state (officially independent from Spain since 1816) as a centralized republic with political power concentrated in its capital of Buenos Aires. On the other side there are the "*Federales*", who wanted to structure Argentina as a federal state consisting of several autonomous provinces. Artigas and most of the Uruguayans were part of the "*Federales*". With the progression of time the two parties started to have different ideas regarding the economy, with the "*Unitarios*" wanting to implement liberal commercial measures, in order to make Buenos Aires a great merchant city, whilst the "*Federales*" were opposed to international commerce and thus wanted to adopt protectionist measures. Buenos Aires was the only major port of Argentina and thus all the goods produced in the interior provinces of the country could be exported abroad only through it. As a result of this situation, the "*Unitarios*" of Buenos Aires could finance their activities thanks to custom duties collected in the port of their capital while the "*Federales*" of the interior provinces were rich in natural resources (including cattle) but had difficulties in selling them abroad. In 1816, taking advantage of the ongoing hostilities between "*Unitarios*" and "*Federales*", Portuguese Brazil invaded Uruguay and transformed the country into the Cisplatine Province. Artigas, who had obtained many victories in the ongoing civil war, continued to fight against the Brazilians until his forces were defeated at the Battle of Tacuarembó on 22 January 1820. In Argentina the civil war ended with the victory of the "*Federales*", who defeated the "*Unitarios*" in a decisive way at the Battle of Cepeda (1 February 1820). The latter was followed by the signing of the Treaty of Pilar, according to which Argentina was to be organized as a confederation of provinces.
- **1821–1825:** Argentina endured some years of political anarchy, with Buenos Aires acting "de facto" as an independent country while some of the interior provinces tried to reach a certain level of unity. Meanwhile, in Brazil, the political situation changed completely. After the outbreak of a liberal revolution in Porto during 1820, King John VI of Portugal left Brazil and promised that his domains would be reorganized as two autonomous kingdoms, Portugal and Brazil, having the same monarch. A constituent assembly, with elected representatives coming from both Portugal and Brazil, was created with the task of "organizing" the transition to the new form of government. Very soon, however, it became apparent that Portugal had no intention of assigning full autonomy to Brazil. As a result, the Brazilian population started to rise up in revolt in Pernambuco and in some other minor centres. Prince Pedro, who had been left in Brazil as regent by his father, became gradually favourable to the idea of seceding from Portugal, since he could count on the loyalty of most of the colonial military

forces. On 7 September 1822 Pedro officially proclaimed the independence of Brazil, which was not recognized by three of his country's provinces nor by the Portuguese troops garrisoned in Uruguay. After obtaining some minor victories over the loyalist Portuguese troops still stationed in Brazil, Emperor Pedro I promulgated the first constitution of Brazil on 20 March 1824. Some months later, on 29 August 1825, Brazilian independence was also officially recognized by King John VI of Portugal.

- **1825–1828:** In Uruguay there was a strong revival of the local pro-independence movement, now guided by Juan Antonio Lavalleja and Manuel Oribe. These, with the decisive support of the Argentine government, organized a constituent congress and proclaimed the independence of their country from the newly-born Empire of Brazil (25 August 1825). The Uruguayan patriots wanted to make the "*Banda Oriental*" one of Argentina's federal provinces and thus soon started to fight against the Brazilian troops stationed in Uruguay. Initially the Uruguayan insurgents obtained a series of victories over their opponents, most notably at the Battle of Sarandí of 12 October 1825. This convinced the Argentines to join the Uruguayans in their struggle. On 10 December 1825 the Empire of Brazil declared war on Argentina and thus the so-called "Cisplatine War" began. Soon after the beginning of hostilities the port of Buenos Aires and the River Plate were completely blockaded by the Brazilian Navy. During 1826 the Argentine-Uruguayan Army expelled the Brazilians from most of the Eastern Bank, except for Montevideo and Colonia del Sacramento. In 1827 the allies invaded the Brazilian state of Rio Grande do Sul from the south and obtained a non-decisive victory at the Battle of Ituzaingó (20 February). Following these events the war entered into a stalemate, since the Argentines were in no conditions to occupy any large portion of southern Brazil while their national economy was in the process of being destroyed by the Brazilian naval blockade. In the end, thanks to the efforts of British diplomacy, the two warring parties reached a compromise and signed the Treaty of Montevideo on 27 August 1828. According to the latter Uruguay became a fully-independent nation, autonomous from both Brazil and Argentina.

- **1829–1835:** Soon after the end of the Cisplatine War, both Argentina and Uruguay entered into a new historical phase characterised by the outbreak of civil wars. In Argentina a new ambitious leader of the "*Federales*", probably the most famous *caudillo* in history, assumed control over the Province of Buenos Aires – Juan Manuel de Rosas. The latter, despite being a federalist, wanted to unify all the provinces of Argentina under his dictatorial control and put in practice an anti-European protectionist economic policy. In 1835 Rosas, after having eliminated most of his internal rivals, became the "absolute ruler" of Argentina. Meanwhile, in Uruguay, two parties emerged and started to dominate the local political life, the conservative party of the "*Blancos*" and the liberal party of the "*Colorados*". Both the "*Blancos*" (Whites) and the "*Colorados*" (Reds) derived their names from the colour of the distinctive cockades worn by their members. The first were particularly strong in the interior areas of Uruguay, had protectionist economic ideas and were allied with the Argentine "*Federales*". The second were based in the Uruguayan capital of Montevideo, had liberal economic ideas and were allied with the Argentine "*Unitarios*". The leader of the "*Blancos*" was Manuel Oribe, while the leader of the "*Colorados*" was Fructuoso Rivera. Both these *Caudillos* had spent their early life fighting against the Brazilian invaders of their country. Initially the "Whites" and the "Reds" found a compromise to avoid the outbreak of a full-scale civil war, in that they agreed to rule Uruguay with a regular alternation. Rivera would have governed first, from 1830 to 1834 and Oribe would have governed next, from 1834 to 1838. During July 1836, however, Rivera broke the pact and rose up in revolt against Oribe. This was the beginning of Uruguay's longest and cruellest civil war, known as the "*Guerra Grande*" or "Great War".

- **1835–1845, Argentina and Paraguay:** Rosas wanted to transform Argentina into the dominant power of South America and thus was extremely active from a military point of view. Inside the borders of his country he organized several campaigns against the native communities living south of Buenos Aires Province in Patagonia, in order to colonize the vast grasslands of the "pampa" that had never been settled before by the Argentine government. Rosas also had to face the internal opposition of the "*Unitarios*", who attempted to depose him on several occasions. The most important leaders of the "*Unitarios*" during the period 1835–1845 were Juan Lavalle and José María Paz. The first fought against Rosas during 1838–1841, while the second revolted against the central government during 1841–1846. Both *Caudillos*, despite being experienced military commanders and despite being able to raise some regular military forces, were decisively defeated by Rosas. The Argentine province that rose up more frequently against Rosas during this period was that of Corrientes, which bordered Paraguay. The latter country remained under Francia's control until 1840, continuing to put in practice a neutral foreign policy. In 1841, however, Carlos Antonio López became the new dictator of Paraguay and gradually started to look outside the borders of his country. Rosas considered both Uruguay and Paraguay as two "rebel" provinces of Argentina and thus had plans for re-conquering them in the future. Fearing that Rosas' military forces could invade his country, López formed an alliance with the province of Corrientes and sent his army to fight under Paz's orders in 1845. In the end, however, the Paraguayan intervention into the Argentine civil wars led to nothing and Rosas' invasion of Paraguay never materialized. During the years 1836–1839 Rosas had to face an external menace also on the north-western borders of his nation, from the powerful but short-lived Peru-Bolivian Confederation. On 19 May 1837, fearing that Bolivia could invade the Argentine provinces of Salta and Tucumán or that they could support his "*Unitarios*" rivals, the dictator declared war on the Peru-Bolivian Confederation and joined the Chileans who were already at war against the latter. Rosas, also due to the harsh natural environment that characterizes the Andean provinces of Salta and Tucumán, contributed very little to the final defeat of the Peru-Bolivian Confederation that was achieved by the Chileans. Rosas' protectionist policies, officially launched in 1835, had important consequences for the international position of Argentina. The *caudillo*, in fact, dreamed of closing the important continental waterway represented by the River Plate to the merchant ships of Great Britain and France. The former was already an "enemy" for Argentina, since she had favoured the end of the Cisplatine War in order to support her main ally in South America (the Empire of Brazil) and had occupied the Malvinas/Falklands in 1833 (the Argentines had always considered these islands as part of their national territory). The latter was an ally of both the Peru-Bolivian Confederation and the Uruguayan "*Colorados*" of Rivera (two regional enemies of Rosas). On 28 March 1838 the French initiated a naval blockade of the River Plate, hoping to obtain the defeat of Rosas by simply closing the port of Buenos Aires to international commerce. The French provided significant funds to the "*Colorados*" of Rivera as well as to the "*Unitarios*" of Lavalle, but in the end their local allies achieved very little and were not able to defeat the military forces of the Argentine dictator. After the Peru-Bolivian Confederation was crushed by the Chileans, it became clear that the French naval blockade of the River Plate was becoming a pointless operation. The French never attempted to land troops on Argentine soil and started to come under an increasing diplomatic pressure exerted from London, since Great Britain did not want to be damaged from an economic point of view by a French military initiative that was obtaining no significant results. In the end, on 29 October 1840, the French warships abandoned Argentine waters and lifted the blockade.

- **1835–1845, Brazil:** In the Empire of Brazil the years 1835–1845 were full of important events and were characterized by a series of local civil wars. In 1826 Pedro I had been crowned King of Portugal following the death of his father John VI. Since the new constitution of Brazil did not permit him to jointly rule Portugal and Brazil, however, Pedro soon abdicated in favour of his infant daughter Maria and returned to Brazil. Pedro's brother Miguel never accepted this state of affairs and thus, counting on the support of most of the Portuguese military forces, in 1828 he deposed Maria and had himself crowned King of Portugal after mounting a coup. In April 1831, having decided that the time had come to fight against his brother Miguel to enforce the rights of his daughter Maria, Pedro I abdicated as Emperor of Brazil and left South America for Portugal, where he was going to fight a civil war against Miguel. Pedro I's successor in Brazil was his infant son Pedro II, who was just five years old in 1831. During the last years of Pedro I's rule the Brazilian liberals had become the most important political group of their country and had started to oppose the decisions of the monarch. When Pedro I left Brazil a "council of regency" had to be created, since the new emperor was too young to rule. This council, consisting of a triumvirate, was dominated by the liberals from the beginning. The new Brazilian government enacted a series of reforms and created the National Guard, but had to face a very strong internal opposition that was guided by the richest landowners. These, acting as proper *Caudillos*, fomented local rebellions that frequently transformed themselves into secessions. The state of Pernambuco rebelled during 1832–1835, followed by Bahia (1835–1838) and Pará (1835–1840). Maranhão rose up in revolt during 1838–1841. All these local revolutions were defeated by the military forces of the central government, mostly because the insurgents were not able to coordinate their efforts. The largest and bloodiest civil war of the so-called "Regency Period", however, took place in the southernmost state of Rio Grande do Sul. This was dominated by a few landowners who had become incredibly rich thanks to cattle breeding. Rio Grande do Sul's male inhabitants were mostly "*gauchos*", i.e. armed cowboys tasked with moving and guarding the cattle of the local landowners. The main product of the territory was the "*charque*" (dried and salted beef), which was also sold outside the borders of Rio Grande do Sul in Argentina and Uruguay. On 20 September 1835 the *Caudillos* of the region rose up in revolt against the central government, by capturing the city of Porto Alegre (capital of their state). The secessionist forces of Rio Grande do Sul were commanded by Bento Gonçalves, an experienced general of the Brazilian Army who had already distinguished himself during the Cisplatine War. The rebels, mostly consisting of gauchos, soon became known as "*Farrapos*" or "Ragamuffins" after the fringed clothes that they used to wear. The *Farrapos* included a large number of black slaves, who worked in the plantations of Rio Grande do Sul and who joined the rebel cause to become free. On 11 September 1836 the revolting state proclaimed its independence as the Riograndense Republic, with Gonçalves as first president. Initially the gauchos obtained a series of victories over the imperial troops sent against them and thus the secessionist movement could spread north through the state of Santa Catarina. Here, on 24 July 1839, the local insurgents proclaimed the secession of their home territory as the Juliana Republic. The latter, however, was quite short-lived since the imperial military forces reconquered most of Santa Catarina by November 1839. In Rio Grande do Sul the so-called "Farrapos War" continued for several more years, since the Ragamuffins could count on the support of the Argentine "*Unitarios*" and of the Uruguayan "*Colorados*" as well as on a brilliant young military commander named Giuseppe Garibaldi. In 1842 overall command of the Brazilian Army was assumed by General Luís Alves de Lima y Silva, who rapidly reorganized in a very effective way the units that were fighting against the rebels. On 1 March 1845, after having been defeated on several occasions, the *Farrapos* agreed to surrender. They were offered a full amnesty in exchange for the full re-incorporation of their state into the Empire of Brazil.

- **1835–1845, Uruguay:** Rivera and his "*Colorados*", after having removed Oribe's government in a coup, formed an alliance with the Argentine province of Corrientes with the objective of defeating Rosas. Rivera, in fact, knew very well that the latter would have soon supported his ally Oribe by providing him with funds and weapons as well as with soldiers. On 31 March 1839, at the Battle of Palo Largo, the "*Federales*" defeated the military forces of Corrientes. Following this clash, Rosas' troops invaded Uruguay from the west but were stopped by Rivera at the Battle of Cagancha (29 December 1839). The unexpected victory of the "*Colorados*" encouraged the Argentine "*Unitarios*" to rise up in revolt against Rosas, and as a result the latter had to fight with most of his military resources against Lavalle during the years 1840–1841. Following Lavalle's defeat, the Argentine dictator decided to put together a large army and to again attack Rivera. His objective was to destroy the military resources of the latter and to restore the "*Blan-*

co" government of Oribe. The decisive clash of this new campaign took place at Arroyo Grande, not far from the border dividing Argentina from Uruguay, on 6 December 1842. This time the military forces of the "*Federales*" and the "*Blancos*" were able to prevail, under the leadership of Oribe. Rivera lost a good portion of his troops and had no choice but to fall back on Montevideo. After a few weeks, on 16 February 1843, the Siege of Montevideo began. The latter, commonly known as the "*Sitio Grande*" or the "Great Siege", was the longest siege operation in the history of modern South America, since it lasted until 1851. From the beginning the siege was a very difficult operation for Oribe, who commanded a mixed force comprising his "*Blancos*" but also sizeable contingents of regular Argentine troops. Rivera, in fact, could count on the political/economic/logistic support of Great Britain and France as well as on the absolute loyalty of Montevideo's numerous cosmopolitan population.

- **1845–1850**: Great Britain and France, understanding that the fall of Montevideo would make Rosas the absolute master of the River Plate, decide to sustain the besieged "*Colorados*" in a more effective way. In 1845 Britain sent the 73rd Regiment of Foot to fight in Montevideo against the besieging army of Oribe. Previously France, in 1843, had sponsored the formation of a large "French Legion" in the city by recruiting volunteers from the French community of Montevideo. The "*Colorados*" military units defending the Uruguayan capital also included an "Italian Legion", commanded by Garibaldi since April 1843. On 18 September 1845 Great Britain and France started a massive naval blockade of the River Plate, with the objective of strangling Rosas' national economy. The Anglo-French fleet, collaborating with a "*Colorado*" flotilla commanded by Garibaldi, soon obtained control over the course of the Uruguay River. On the course of the Paraná River the situation was different since Rosas had fortified the banks of the waterway before the arrival of the European vessels. The allies wanted to sail up river to transport large amounts of supplies to the "*Unitarios*" of Corrientes and to the Paraguayans, who were fighting against Rosas. The latter could not allow his northern enemies to be equipped with new weapons as was happening for Rivera's troops in Montevideo, or the whole of northern Argentina would have revolted against his rule. The most important Argentine fortification on the Paraná River was located in a place named Vuelta de Obligado, at a point where the waterway is just 700 metres wide and where the turning made sailing ship navigation quite difficult. The Argentines deployed some of their best units in the area and built four artillery batteries with heavy pieces at Vuelta de Obligado. In addition, they placed three chains across the course of the Paraná River. The 11 warships of the Anglo-French fleet attacked the Argentine defences on 20 November 1845, but they met an incredibly strong resistance. At the end of the clash the allies had been able to break the chains and to destroy all the enemy batteries, but their warships were so severely damaged that they had to stop at Vuelta de Obligado for repairs for 40 days. During the early weeks of 1846 the Anglo-French fleet finally reached Paraguay and Corrientes, after having fought some other riverine actions against Rosas' stubborn military forces. Once in the Paraguayan capital of Asunción, however, the allies learned that the local government had no intention of attacking Argentina with a sizeable army. After the failure of this expedition on the Paraná, Great Britain and France continued their blockade of the River Plate for some more years. In 1849, however, France put an end to the hostilities with Rosas and was followed by Great Britain in 1850. According to the agreement reached between Argentina and the allies, Rosas was to withdraw his troops from the siege of Montevideo while the "*Colorados*" were to disband their legions formed by foreign volunteers.

- **1851–1852**: After many years of absolute rule, the personal power of Rosas in Argentina started to be weakened by a series of events. First of all, a new capable leader emerged from the ranks of the "*Federales*", Justo José de Urquiza. The latter had previously been one of Rosas' main military commanders and was particularly strong in his home province of Entre Ríos. Urquiza wanted to become the new leader of the "*Federales*" and thus was a strong internal rival for Rosas. The British and the French, who had never fully renounced to the idea of deposing Rosas, understood that by supporting Urquiza in his ambitious plans they could finally defeat their worst enemy in the River Plate. Having no intention of sending large expeditionary forces to South America, the two European powers started to work on the formation of a local anti-Rosas alliance. The British diplomats convinced Pedro II of Brazil, who was now free from his "Council of Regency" since 1840, to mobilize his large military forces against Rosas. On 29 May 1851 the diplomatic efforts of Great Britain finally reached their objectives. The "*Colorados*" of Rivera, the Argentine province of Entre Ríos and the Empire of Brazil signed a military alliance in Montevideo with the objective of defeating Rosas in a definitive way. On 19 July 1851 Urquiza invaded Uruguay from Entre Ríos and marched against Oribe's army that was still besieging Montevideo after eight long years. This was the beginning of a new conflict, known as the "Platine War". After 13,000 Brazilian soldiers also entered Uruguay, the leader of the "*Blancos*" decided to surrender on 8 October 1851. The "*Sitio Grande*" and the "*Guerra Grande*" were over, Rivera and his "*Colorados*" had won. The Argentine troops who were still under Oribe's orders decided to change sides and joined Urquiza's troops. Following these events, the new government of Uruguay came under a strong Brazilian influence and sent its best military forces against Rosas. On 3 February 1852 the decisive clash between the Argentine dictator and his enemies was fought at Caseros. Here the "*Ejército Grande*" or "Great Army" of the Allies (19,000 pro-Urquiza Argentines, 3,500 Brazilians and 1,500 Uruguayans) decisively defeated a force of 22,000 soldiers supporting Rosas.

- **1852–1858**: Following his great victory at Caseros, Urquiza became the absolute ruler of Argentina. He sponsored the promulgation of a new federal constitution and reorganized his country as the "Argentine Confederation". Urquiza, as could be expected, favoured in every possible way the interior provinces of Argentina and in particular his home territory of Entre Ríos. This caused great discontent in Buenos Aires, where the local exponents of the middle classes were against the new federal constitution of the Argentine state. Urquiza wanted to obtain direct control over the collection of custom duties that took place in Buenos Aires and wanted to deprive the latter of her "provincial" status (making the city a simple federal capital). These measures were unacceptable for the "*porteños*" (the inhabitants of Buenos Aires), who revolted against the Argentine Confederation on 11 September 1852 and proclaimed the independence of their own province as the new "State of Buenos Aires". During the last months of 1852 Urquiza's forces marched on Buenos Aires and besieged the city, but after a few weeks they were obliged to leave the territory of the secessionist state. In 1854 the State of Buenos Aires promulgated its own constitution. Meanwhile, it continued to prosper thanks to international commerce. For a few years Urquiza did not attempt to invade the State of Buenos Aires again, but some minor skirmishes continued to occur along the border dividing the two Argentine states. In Uruguay, after the end of the "*Guerra Grande*", the leading members of the "*Colorados*" and of the "*Blancos*" attempted a national reconciliation. A new "fusionist" policy was implemented, according to which members of both parties were to collaborate together for the prosperity of the whole nation. In 1858, however, there was a rebellion of "*Colorados*" against the new "mixed" government that was crushed with violence. This led to the beginning of a new phase of civil conflicts fought between the "*Blancos*" and the "*Colorados*".

- **1859–1862**: In May 1859, fearing that other provinces of the Argentine Confederation could join Buenos Aires, Urquiza mobilized his military forces to invade the latter. The first important clash of this new civil war was fought at Cepeda on 23 October 1859. Here the military forces of the State of Buenos Aires, commanded by Bartolomé Mitre, were defeated but not in a decisive way. Following this battle, the two warring sides decided to sign a truce ahead of concluding a definitive peace treaty. Buenos Aires agreed to be re-incorporated into the Argentine Confederation in exchange for a complete revision of the constitution inspired by Urquiza, that would have preserved her traditional economic privileges. In reality, the secessionist government of Buenos Aires had accepted the truce just to gain some precious time in view of a new, and hopefully decisive, military campaign. This finally materialized in the summer of 1861, when the new governor of Buenos Aires, Mitre, assembled an army to fight against Urquiza. The new campaign ended on 17 September 1861, with the decisive Battle of Pavón. This saw the troops from Buenos Aires decisively defeat the army of the Argentine Confederation. With his victory at Pavón, Mitre re-unified Argentina as a single republic and became the latter's president. In 1862 Carlos Antonio López, after having been for long time dictator of Paraguay, died. He was succeeded by his son Francisco Solano López, who dreamed of making his country the most powerful nation of South America. Unlike his father, who had mostly avoided being involved into major military conflicts to preserve the flourishing economy of his republic, the new Paraguayan president planned to create a "sub-Amazonian empire" by conquering large territories belonging to Brazil and Argentina. The dictator was also interested in gaining direct access to the sea for his landlocked country. To achieve this objective, he started to play a role in the internal politics of Uruguay by financially supporting the "*Blancos*".

- **1863–1865**: On 19 April 1863 the new leader of the "*Colorados*", Venancio Flores, launched a new revolution in Uruguay known as "*Cruzada Libertadora*" or "Liberating Crusade". Flores, a personal friend of the Argentine president Mitre, wanted to remove the new "*Blanco*" government that had been installed in Uruguay following the events of 1858. In doing so he was supported by both Argentina and Brazil, since the latter countries were extremely worried about the possibility that Uruguay could become a protectorate of Francisco Solano López's expanding Paraguay. The new civil war fought between the "*Colorados*" and the "*Blancos*" soon entered a stalemate, since the former obtained some successes in the countryside while the latter had firm control over the major urban centres. As a result of this situation, after the failure of some diplomatic negotiations, on 12 October 1864 the Empire of Brazil invaded Uruguay in order to support Flores. The Brazilian Army quite rapidly defeated the "*Blancos*", forcing them to fall back on the fortified city of Paysandú. The latter resisted for a month (2 December 1864 – 2 January 1865) the siege conducted jointly by the Brazilians and by the "*Colorados*", in the hope of receiving some reinforcements from Paraguay. In the end, however, the "*Blancos*" were completely defeated and Flores became the master of Uruguay thanks to the decisive support of Brazil. While this conflict, commonly known as the "Uruguayan War", ended, a new and larger one began in the River Plate region. Francisco Solano López's Paraguay, in fact, declared war on Brazil on 13 December 1864. In March 1865 the new conflict, known as the "Paraguayan War" or as the "War of the Triple Alliance", became even larger when Paraguay also attacked Argentina. On 1 May 1865 Pedro II's Brazil, Mitre's Argentina and Flores' Uruguay signed the anti-Paraguayan "Triple Alliance". This event marked the beginning of the end for the expansionist dreams of the last *caudillo* from the River Plate region, Francisco Solano López, who was finally defeated and killed by the allies in 1870.

Military conflicts in the Andean and Caribbean regions, 1825–1865

- **1825–1829:** After expelling the last Spanish troops from mainland South America, the Gran Colombian Army continued to garrison Bolivia. The latter became an independent republic in 1825, under the protection of the Gran Colombian Confederation. The Peruvians, however, nurtured the ambition of occupying Bolivia since the latter had always been annexed with Peru during the Spanish colonial period. Meanwhile Gran Colombia entered a phase of political instability, due to the secessionist ambitions of Venezuela. The latter was under the control of José Antonio Páez, who was one of the most important commanders of the Gran Colombian Army and the most prominent "*caudillo*" of Venezuela. In 1826 Páez rebelled against the central government of Gran Colombia, initiating a revolt that became known as "La Cosiata". This was suppressed, but Gran Colombia continued to be shattered by the Venezuelan secessionist plans during the following years. Also Ecuador and Panama started to nurture the ambition of becoming independent nations. In 1828, hoping to take advantage of Gran Colombia's military weakness, Peru invaded Bolivia. The local Gran Colombian garrison was defeated and forced to evacuate the country, an event that marked the beginning of the so-called "Gran Colombia-Peru War". The conflict saw a Peruvian invasion of Ecuador on land and a Peruvian blockade of the Gran Colombian Pacific coastline at sea. On 27 February 1829, at the decisive Battle of Tarqui, the Gran Colombian Army defeated the Peruvian one. The conflict came to an end with the signing of the Guayaquil Treaty, according to which Bolivia ceased to be a Gran Colombian protectorate but Ecuador remained part of Gran Colombia.
- **1830:** The Gran Colombian Confederation ceases to exist, due to the secessions of Ecuador (13 May) and Venezuela (22 September). Both countries became independent republics, the first under the guidance of Juan José Flores and the second under the guidance of José Antonio Páez. Also Panama tried to secede from Gran Colombia, but without success. In 1831 what remained of Gran Colombia, i.e. Colombia and Panama, assumed the new official denomination of "*Nueva Grenada*".
- **1835–1839:** During 1835–1836 Peru was shattered by a bloody civil war fought between conservatives and liberals. The latter could count on the support of Bolivia, whose president since 1829 was the experienced Peruvian general Andrés de Santa Cruz. The Peruvian liberals and the Bolivian president wanted to unite Peru and Bolivia into a single state. This became possible after Santa Cruz invaded Peru with the Bolivian Army and after Agustín Gamarra, one of the most capable Peruvian military leaders, joined the cause of the Peruvian liberals. Following the defeat of the Peruvian conservatives, Peru and Bolivia were united together in 1836 as a new state that was known as the "Peru-Bolivian Confederation". This, from an administrative point of view, consisted of three autonomous entities, the "Northern Peruvian State", the "Southern Peruvian State" and the "Bolivian State". Gamarra was opposed to the division of Peru into two semi-autonomous states and thus soon started to lead the opposition to Santa Cruz (who was the supreme leader of the Peru-Bolivian Confederation). In 1836 Chile decided to declare war on the Peru-Bolivian state, since the latter represented a serious menace to Chilean territorial integrity. The Chileans welcomed Gamarra and his supporters, organizing with them a first expedition against Peru-Bolivia that led to no significant results. In 1837 the anti-Santa Cruz coalition was joined by Argentina, but the latter's participation in the ongoing conflict had a purely defensive posture. In 1837 the Chilean Army and the Peruvian forces of Gamarra invaded the Peru-Bolivian Confederation on a large scale. After several months of fighting, on 20 January 1839 they finally defeated the military forces of Santa Cruz in a decisive way at the Battle of Yungay. Following the latter, the Peru-Bolivian Confederation was dissolved. Peru was re-unified under the leadership of Gamarra, while Bolivia entered a period of political chaos.
- **1841:** Gamarra, hoping to take advantage from the weakness of Bolivia, invaded the latter country with the Peruvian Army. Following this event José Ballivián, an experienced general, took the leadership of his country by terminating the ongoing Bolivian civil conflict. On 18 November, against all odds, the Bolivian Army of Ballivián obtained a decisive victory over the Peruvians at the Battle of Ingavi (during which Gamarra was killed). The latter clash secured Bolivia's independence from Peru.
- **1845–1849:** Ecuador and Venezuela were shattered by civil wars. In Ecuador Juan José Flores, after having dominated the political life of the country for a long time, was removed from the presidency in 1845. During 1846 he tried to regain his power with the support of Spain, but without success. In Venezuela a major civil war broke out in 1848 and was fought between the conservatives and the liberals. The conflict ends with the victory of the latter in 1849 and with the exile of the conservative leader José Antonio Páez.
- **1851–1854:** Colombia is devastated by two bloody civil wars, which are fought between conservatives and liberals. The country enters a period of political anarchy.
- **1858–1860, Ecuador:** In 1858, taking advantage of the state of civil war that had existed in Ecuador since 1856, the Peruvians invaded the Ecuadorian territory from the south. This marked the beginning of the so-called "Peru-Ecuadorian War", which saw a Peruvian naval blockade of the Ecuadorian coastline and the Peruvian occupation

of Guayaquil (Ecuador's most important city at the time). The Peruvians took advantage of the Ecuadorian political weakness, since Ecuador was divided into two parts by 1858. The northern one including Quito and the southern one including Guayaquil, which fought each other for economic interests. The Peru-Ecuadorian War ended in 1860 with the victory of Peru and of the pro-Peru Ecuadorian faction based in Guayaquil. Ecuador was forced to sign the Treaty of Mapasingue, according to which a large portion of southern Ecuador was annexed by Peru. Despite this, however, during 1860 Ecuador was re-unified under the leadership of the faction that dominated in Quito.

- **1859–1863, Venezuela:** The Venezuelans were shattered by the bloodiest civil war of their history, the so-called "Federal War". The latter was fought between the conservatives having centralist ideas and the liberals who wanted to transform Venezuela into a confederation of autonomous regional states. The conflict ended with the victory of the liberals and with the adoption of a new federalist constitution for Venezuela.
- **1860–1862, Colombia:** In 1860 a new civil conflict broke out in Colombia between conservatives and liberals, known as "*Guerra de las Soberanías*". The conservatives had centralist ideas, while the liberals wanted to transform Colombia into a confederation of autonomous regional states. The war saw the temporary intervention of Ecuador in favour of the Colombian liberals, which led to no positive results for the Ecuadorians (who attempted to annex some border areas of Colombia). The "*Guerra de las Soberanías*" ended in 1862 with a decisive victory for the liberals and with the adoption of a new federalist constitution for Colombia. According to the latter, Colombia ceased to have a centralized regular army.
- **1864–1866:** During the 1860s Queen Isabel II of Spain nurtured the ambition of reconquering some areas of what had been the glorious Spanish Empire in the Americas. The Spanish government had never recognized the independence of several American republics and in particular of Peru, since the latter had been for centuries the richest and most important of the Spanish colonies. In the last months of 1862 Spain organized a scientific expedition to the waters of South America, officially with the objective of conducting research in that part of the world. In reality, the naval expedition had the covert purpose of reinforcing the financial and legal claims that several Spanish citizens living in the Americas were directing against the American republics. The Spanish government, in fact, wanted to use these financial and legal claims as a potential "*casus belli*" to intervene against the South American countries. The Spanish naval expedition consisted of four warships, two steam frigates, one corvette and one schooner. The Spanish vessels arrived in the Chilean port of Valparaiso on 18 April 1863. Here they were received very cordially by the local authorities before deciding to move to Peru in July. The Spanish naval squadron was well received also in the Peruvian port of Callao, despite the fact that Spain had never recognized the independence of Peru. After sailing along the Peruvian coastline, the Spanish warships moved to San Francisco in California. During their visits in the ports of Valparaiso and Callao the Spaniards had the opportunity to study the local defences with a view to a future attack or blockade. The Spanish government, in fact, had the intention of re-taking control of some important Pacific port of South America, which would have enabled Spain to control the lucrative sea routes connecting her colony of the Philippines with the Americas.

On 4 August 1863 the incident that the Spaniards were waiting for took place in Peru, in a farm located at Talambo. Here some Spanish residents were involved in disturbances with the local population and one of them was killed. The episode was a perfect "*casus belli*" for the Spaniards and thus from San Francisco the naval squadron was sent back to Peru. The commander of the Spanish naval forces demanded an official apology and economic reparations to be made by the Peruvian government to the Spanish nationals who had been hurt. The Peruvians responded that the "Talambo Incident" was just an episode of and internal police matter that had to be handled according to their own national laws. The Spaniards made tension escalate by demanding the immediate payment of the debts that Peru had with Spain since 1821, something that was perceived as an insult by the Peruvian authorities. On 14 April 1864, in retaliation for Peru's refusal to pay any form of indemnity for the "Talambo Incident", the Spanish fleet occupied the poorly defended Chincha Islands. The latter were part of the Peruvian national territory and were extremely profitable from an economic point of view because they were rich in guano. The latter, in the central decades of the 19th century, was the most effective fertilizer in the world. It was exported to many different countries and could be sold at high prices. The Chincha Islands, being located quite near to the coastline of central Peru, would have been a naval base for the Spaniards from which the most important ports of Pacific South America could be attacked. The Chncha Islands produced almost 60% of the Peruvian government's annual revenue and thus the Peruvians could not renounce them without fighting.

The Spaniards were convinced that the Peruvian military forces would be no match for them, especially the naval ones. As a result, they initiated a blockade of the principal Peruvian ports with the objective of disrupting commerce and of fostering a high level of resentment in the civilian population. Another four warships were sent to reinforce the Spanish fleet operating in South American waters, something that made anti-Spanish sentiments explode in several countries of South America. All the former Spanish colonies having access to the Pacific, in fact, felt menaced by the presence of a large Spanish fleet just off their coastlines. Several contemporary political observers feared that Spain could try to restore a form of colonial empire in America and thus started to work on the creation of a large anti-Spanish coalition. Given this climate of tension and suspicion, it was not surprising that, when a Spanish warship stopped at a Chilean port for coal, the Chileans declared that latter could not be sold to a belligerent nation since it was a war supply. The Chilean coaling embargo was taken by the Spaniards as a proof that Chile was no longer neutral in the ongoing war. The Spanish view was confirmed when two Peruvian steamers left the port of Valparaiso full of Chilean volunteers and weapons. As a result of these events, four Spanish warships were dispatched to Chile and arrived at Valparaiso on 17 September

1865. A few days later, war was declared between Spain and Chile.

The Spaniards did not have any military contingent on their warships and thus could not attempt any landing, they could only impose a naval blockade of the main Chilean ports, as they had already done with the Peruvian ones. The coastlines of Peru and Chile, however, were too long to be properly blockaded by the few vessels that the Spaniards had in South American waters. As a result, the Spanish warships concentrated on blockading only Callao in Peru and Valparaiso in Chile. The blockade of these two ports caused such economic damage to both the American republics and the foreign naval powers like Great Britain and the United States that Spain soon came under strong diplomatic pressure aimed at removing it. The Spaniards, in any case, had greatly underestimated the combat capabilities of the Peruvian Navy and of the Chilean Navy. On 26 November 1865, at the Battle of Papudo, the Chilean corvette "*Esmeralda*" captured the Spanish schooner "*Covadonga*"; this defeat was particularly humiliating for the Spaniards, who started to abandon their previous confidence.

On the same day as the Battle of Papudo a new government took power in Peru, which was strongly determined to defeat the Spanish naval forces in order to reconquer the Chincha Islands. The new Peruvian government signed an alliance with Chile and declared war on Spain. The anti-Spanish alliance was joined by Ecuador on 30 January 1866 and by Bolivia on 22 March 1866. Ecuador and Bolivia did not have effective fleets like those of Peru and Chile, but their declaration of war on Spain meant that all the Pacific ports of South America were now closed to the Spanish vessels. The Spaniards responded to these events by trying to fight a decisive engagement with the combined Peruvian-Chilean fleet. Such a naval battle took place on 7 February 1866 at Abtao, a well-protected inlet located near the Gulf of Chiloé in southern Chile. Reluctant to enter shallow waters and realizing that a long-range gun duel would have led to nothing positive for them, the Spaniards withdrew from the clash without having damaged any of the enemy warships.

With the progression of time the Spanish naval squadron became isolated and short of supplies, something that obliged the Spanish commanders to take the initiative before the Peruvian-Chilean fleet could retaliate. On 31 March 1866 the Spanish fleet shelled and burned the port of Valparaiso, destroying Chile's merchant fleet. Destroying a defenceless port, however, had very little positive consequences for the Spaniards, who were in no condition to continue the hostilities for long time. Hoping to bring the hostilities to an end by achieving an important symbolic victory, the Spanish warships headed to Callao. The latter, unlike Valparaiso, was well fortified. On 2 May 1866 the Spanish fleet, forming a V-shaped line of attack, entered the bay of Callao with six of its seven warships. The Spaniards bombarded the Peruvian defences, but the fire coming from the latter was quite effective. The frigate "*Villa de Madrid*" was hit by a 450-pound projectile that destroyed its boilers; the steam frigate "*Berenguela*" was pierced side-to-side at the waterline by a 300-pound projectile after having silenced several Peruvian guns; the frigate "*Almansa*" was hit and its powder room exploded. Despite their losses the Spaniards continued to fight with great valour, destroying several Peruvian batteries. The Peruvians feared that their enemies could attempt a landing and thus had entrenched 3,000 soldiers outside their coastal fortifications. These men were bombarded by the Spanish vessels but the landing never materialized. After several hours of battle, during which a few Peruvian warships tried to approach the Spanish fleet but without success, the Spaniards decided to cease fire and to retreat from Callao. Most of the Spanish warships were severely damaged and dozens of Spanish sailors were wounded. The Battle of Callao was an indecisive clash, since the Spaniards destroyed most of the enemy defences but suffered severe losses. Despite this, however, both sides claimed victory. After the Battle of Callao, it became clear to the Spanish government that its plans for the reconquest of any South American territory were completely utopian. The American republics were too strong to be defeated by Spain alone, and since the early months of 1866 they could also count on the support of the United States, because the US Civil War had ended. With all the Pacific ports located south of Colombia closed to them for coaling and provisioning, the Spanish fleet had no choice but to abandon South American waters, after having evacuated the Chincha Islands. The latter were soon re-occupied by the Peruvians, while the Spanish vessels returned to their homeland via the Philippines (completing a circumnavigation of the globe to do so).

The Brazilian Army

History and organization

The Empire of Brazil inherited from the Portuguese colonial administration a well-organized and quite large military apparatus, which remained practically intact during the years 1822–1825 that saw Brazil becoming completely autonomous from Portugal. The Portuguese exported to Brazil the traditional military system that existed in their motherland for some centuries, which was based on three main "categories" or "lines" of troops. Each of colonial Brazil's provinces, in fact, had the following: a certain number of regular/professional military units that were recruited on a local basis and formed the "*Primeira Linha*" or "First Line"; a certain number of "*Milicia*" units consisting of semi-professional militia corps tasked with performing police duties inside their home territories, which formed the "*Segunda Linha*" or "Second Line"; a certain number of "*Ordenança*" units consisting of non-professional militiamen who could be called to serve only in case of emergency and whose corps existed only on paper, who made up the "*Terceira Linha*" or "Third Line". During colonial times the units of the "*Milicia*" were much better organized and trained compared with those of the "*Ordenança*". They, in fact, usually wore some sort of uniform and received their weapons from the various provincial governments. The "*Milicia*" was usually recruited from the urban centres, while the "*Ordenança*" was recruited from the rural areas. All able-bodied men aged 15–60

Brazilian uniforms in 1823 (model 1816), from left to right: horse artilleryman, officer of the foot artillery, grenadier and officer of the grenadiers.

could be called to serve in the "*Ordenança*". Their names were included into special lists that were kept by the military officers deployed in each province. When mobilized, the single companies of the "*Ordenança*" were assembled together into groups of fifteen, commanded by a retired senior officer who had previously served in the regular troops. Generally speaking, the members of the "*Ordenança*" were little more than armed civilians. The quality of the soldiers of the "*Milicia*", instead, could vary a lot. Some militia units recruited from the wealthy social groups of the major cities could be of good quality, while other corps formed in the smaller centres could be of no military use. The regular military units of the various provinces did not include black soldiers, but the "*Milicia*", instead, comprised several corps of free blacks. The latter were known as "*Henriques*" from the name of Henrique Dias, a free black soldier who had been the main Brazilian hero of the Dutch-Portuguese War (1602–1663).

After Portugal was invaded by Napoleon in 1807, the Portuguese royal family left Europe for Brazil. Here King John VI did his best to improve the general quality of the locally-recruited regular military forces. In 1808 he transformed the squadron tasked with acting as the mounted bodyguard of the Viceroy of Brazil into a heavy cavalry regiment with eight companies (the Cavalry Regiment of Rio de Janeiro). He also created a foot bodyguard for the defence of his person, consisting of 25 men wearing ceremonial uniforms and known as "*Archeiros da Guarda Real*" or "Archers of the Royal Guard".

The infantry battalion of "*Henriques*" existing in the capital of Rio de Janeiro was expanded to become a regiment and, in 1809, a first corps of mounted artillery was created together with a small unit of artificers. John VI also separated the territory of Rio Grande do Sul from that of Santa Catarina, making it a new province. The latter would be garrisoned by the following regular troops: one battalion of *Caçadores* (light infantry) and one regiment of dragoons. In 1811 the Portuguese monarch inaugurated the Royal Military Academy of Rio de Janeiro. John VI also reorganized the Portuguese marines – now based in Brazil – as the "Corps of the Royal Navy Brigade in Brazil" with three battalions having eight companies each. In 1816, for the invasion of Uruguay, John VI decided to organize an expeditionary force of metropolitan units in Portugal that was later sent to Rio de Janeiro. This, known as "Auxiliary Division of Royal Volunteers", consisted of four light infantry battalions as well as of six cavalry squadrons and two companies of artillery. These units were made up of volunteers who were veterans of the Napoleonic Wars and who were extremely loyal to the Portuguese monarchy. Once in Brazil the infantry of the Auxiliary Division was re-structured into two brigades with one line regiment and one light battalion each (the former with 10 companies, the latter with 6 companies). In 1818 the grenadier companies of the three infantry battalions existing in Rio de Janeiro were assembled together to form a separate Battalion of Grenadiers, having special guard status.

Brazilian uniforms in 1822 (model 1816), from left to right: officer of the caçadores, caçador, cavalryman and foot militiaman of the 2nd Line.

The formation of the Brazilian Army, 1822–1831

After John VI left Brazil for Portugal, his son Pedro, who had been nominated regent in Rio de Janeiro, started to organize some new military forces on whose loyalty he could count, in case the process he was planning to achieve the independence of Brazil would have seen the outbreak of a full-scale civil war. First of all he created a Civic Guard for the defence of his new court, which would comprise four infantry battalions and two cavalry squadrons. Later, in October 1822, Pedro raised his own battalions of "*Henriques*" (one of infantry and one of artillery). The Prince Regent was sure that all the Brazilian regular troops would side with him after the proclamation of independence, but during the previous years his father had transferred some Portuguese metropolitan units to Brazil and these would surely have opposed his plans in some of the major cities like Rio de Janeiro and Bahia. For this reason, he needed to form some new units that would fight for him, without hesitation, against the Portuguese contingents stationed in Brazil. Luckily for Prince Pedro, the Auxiliary Division of Royal Volunteers was garrisoned in the Cisplatine Province and thus was far from his capital of Rio de Janeiro. On 10 November 1822 the Prince Regent grouped all the Brazilian regular military forces garrisoning his capital just outside Rio de Janeiro and selected 800 men from the various corps. These soldiers, chosen according to their loyalty towards Pedro, were assembled into a new "special" grenadier battalion having six companies. When the Prince Regent officially proclaimed the independence of Brazil, the new unit was sent against the Portuguese troops that were stationed in Bahia (the latter was the main stronghold of the loyalists in Brazil). The chosen corps fought extremely well in Bahia and after its return to Rio de Janeiro, on 18 January 1823, it finally received its official denomination of "Battalion of the Emperor" together with the honour of acting as the foot guard of Pedro I. The unit was later sent to Uruguay, in order to replace the Auxiliary Division in the local garrison (since the latter had returned to Portugal). The Battalion of the Emperor continued to exist as an elite corps until 1831, when it was disbanded following the abdication of Pedro I in favour of his son Pedro II.

Brazilian uniforms in 1823 (model 1816), from left to right: officer of the caçadores, caçador, officer of the 2nd Line and officer of the 3rd Line.

Brazilian uniforms in 1825, from left to right: cavalry militiaman of the 2nd Line, caçador in parade dress and caçador in campaign dress.

Brazilian uniforms in 1825, from left to right: trooper of the cavalry, officer of the cavalry, militia cavalry officer of the 2nd Line, naval artilleryman.

After it became clear that the Prince Regent would proclaim the independence of Brazil, several of the country's provinces raised volunteer corps to support Pedro. São Paulo, in particular, sent to the court a squadron of mounted volunteers whose officers were mostly aristocrats and whose soldiers were former officers of the militia. The Prince Regent, needing to have a mounted bodyguard consisting of loyal individuals having some combat experience, transformed this squadron of volunteers into his "Guard of Honour" on 1 December 1822. The new unit mustered three heavy cavalry squadrons whose members, employing dragoon equipment, were recruited from the young aristocrats and well-to-do gentlemen of Brazil who were loyal to the new regime. Like the Battalion of the Emperor, the Imperial Guard of Honour was disbanded, in 1832, soon after its creator Pedro I left Brazil for Portugal. In 1826 the Corps of the Royal Navy Brigade in Brazil was reorganized as the new Imperial Naval Artillery Brigade, consisting of two battalions with six companies each; in 1828 the denomination of the unit was changed again – becoming "Naval Artillery Corps" – together with its internal structure that was now to comprise two battalions with eight companies each.

Fearing that his father John VI could organize a large military expedition to reconquer Brazil, Pedro tried to recruit substantial numbers of European mercenaries in order to augment the level of combat experience of the military forces supporting his cause. At that time Europe was full of veterans of the Napoleonic Wars who were in search of new employment and who could have been interested in moving to South America to earn a living. Pedro sent his agents to Germany and was able to recruit a good number of mercenaries. These, on 18 January 1822, were assembled into a separate "*Corpo de Estraingeiros*" or "Corps of Foreigners". This, after some more recruiting operations, came to consist of one heavy infantry brigade with two grenadier battalions and one light infantry brigade with two *Caçador* battalions. These units were united with the other corps of the newly-created Brazilian Army in December 1824. Initially the German professional soldiers distinguished themselves for their good discipline and for their excellent combat capabilities, to the point that in 1825, following the outbreak of the Cisplatine War, a squadron of lancers was raised from the German emigrants living in Rio Grande do Sul. In 1827, following the success of the German mercenaries, Pedro I sent his agents also to Ireland in order to recruit some more men. 2,700 volunteers responded to the call and agreed to move to South America with their families in order to become military colonists.

Once in Brazil, however, the Irishmen finally understood that they had not been recruited to settle and defend some agricultural lands but to be employed as mercenary profession-

Brazilian uniforms in 1825, from left to right: sergeant of the German grenadiers, private of the German caçadores, private of the German grenadiers and officer of the German caçadores in stable dress.

al soldiers. In June 1828, after an episode of indiscipline that had been punished severely by Pedro I, the German soldiers of the Corps of Foreigners stationed in Rio de Janeiro mutinied and rebelled against the Brazilian authorities. They were soon joined by the Irishmen who had recently arrived in the city, who had refused to enlist as soldiers and who were dying of starvation with their families. The Brazilian capital then endured some days of terror, during what became known as the "Mercenary Revolt". Pedro I, to avoid the complete destruction of Rio de Janeiro, had to ask for the help of the British and French warships that were anchored in the port of his capital. In the end the mutiny was crushed only after 400 British and 600 French sailors disembarked from their warships to fight against the infuriated mercenaries. Following this terrible episode all the mercenary units in Brazilian service were progressively disbanded, except for the Squadron of German Lancers that continued to exist until 1831.

On 1 December 1824, after having expelled the last metropolitan Portuguese troops from Brazil, Pedro I could finally give a definitive and proper structure to his military forces that officially became the Brazilian Army. The various regular infantry corps of the colonial army were reorganized as follows:

- The Grenadier Battalion became the 1st Grenadier Battalion
- The 1st Grenadier Battalion of the Corps of Foreigners became the 2nd Grenadier Battalion
- The 2nd Grenadier Battalion of the Corps of Foreigners became the 3rd Grenadier Battalion
- The 1st *Caçador* Battalion of Rio de Janeiro became the 1st *Caçador* Battalion
- The 2nd *Caçador* Battalion of Rio de Janeiro became the 2nd *Caçador* Battalion
- The 3rd *Caçador* Battalion of Rio de Janeiro became the 3rd *Caçador* Battalion
- The 4th *Caçador* Battalion of Rio de Janeiro became the 4th *Caçador* Battalion
- The 1st *Caçador* Battalion of São Paulo became the 5th *Caçador* Battalion
- The 2nd *Caçador* Battalion of São Paulo became the 6th *Caçador* Battalion
- The Infantry Legion of São Paulo became the 7th *Caçador* Battalion
- The *Caçador* Battalion of Santa Catarina became the 8th *Caçador* Battalion
- The Infantry and Artillery Battalion of Curitiba became the 9th *Caçador* Battalion
- The 1st Battalion of Libertos (free blacks) of Montevideo became the 10th *Caçadores* Battalion
- The 2nd Battalion of Libertos (free blacks) of Montevideo became the 11th *Caçadores* Battalion
- The Infantry and Cavalry Companies of Espiritu Santu became the 12th *Caçadores* Battalion
- The 1st *Caçador* Battalion of Bahia became the 13th *Caçadores* Battalion
- The 2nd *Caçador* Battalion of Bahia became the 14th *Caçadores* Battalion
- The 3rd *Caçador* Battalion of Bahia became the 15th *Caçadores* Battalion
- The Infantry Battalion of Alagoas became the 16th *Caçadores* Battalion
- The 1st *Caçador* Battalion of Pernambuco became the 17th *Caçadores* Battalion
- The 2nd *Caçador* Battalion of Pernambuco became the 18th *Caçadores* Battalion
- The 3rd *Caçador* Battalion of Pernambuco became the 19th *Caçadores* Battalion
- The Infantry Battalion of Paraiba became the 20th *Caçadores* Battalion
- The Infantry Companies of Piuaí became the 21st *Caçadores* Battalion
- The Infantry Companies of Rio Grande do Norte became the 22nd *Caçadores* Battalion
- The Infantry Companies of Ceará became the 23rd *Caçadores* Battalion
- The Infantry Companies of Maranhão became the 24th *Caçadores* Battalion
- The Infantry Companies of Pará became the 25th *Caçadores* Battalion
- The 1st *Caçador* Battalion of the Corps of Foreigners became the 26th *Caçadores* Battalion
- The 2nd *Caçador* Battalion of the Corps of Foreigners became the 27th *Caçadores* Battalion

Following the contemporary Portuguese model, the 3 grenadier battalions had ten companies each while the 27 *Caçador* battalions had six companies each. It should be noted that, despite their light infantry denomination, the various units of *Caçadores* were normal line infantry corps. All the 30 battalions consisted of white soldiers, except for the two ones raised from the free blacks of recently-conquered Uruguay. The three grenadier battalions were grouped into an autonomous brigade, which had elite status but did not comprise the independent "Battalion of the Emperor". In 1825 a new light infantry battalion, recruited in Sergipe, was added to those listed above. By 1830 all the four German battalions had been disbanded and thus only one grenadier battalion remained (which was disbanded in 1831). The various regular cavalry corps of the colonial army were reorganized as follows:

- The Cavalry Regiment of Rio de Janeiro became the 1st Cavalry Regiment
- The Cavalry Regiment of Minas Gerais became the 2nd Cavalry Regiment
- The Cavalry Legion of São Paulo became the 3rd Cavalry Regiment
- The Cavalry Squadrons of São Pedro (Rio Grande do Sul) became the 4th Cavalry Regiment
- The Dragoon Regiment of Rio Pardo (Rio Grande do Sul) became the 5th Cavalry Regiment
- The Dragoon Regiment of Montevideo (Uruguay) became the 6th Cavalry Regiment
- The Dragoon Regiment of Paysandú (Uruguay) became the 7th Cavalry Regiment

Each of the mounted regiments consisted of three squadrons. It is interesting to note that four units out of seven were recruited from the "gaucho" provinces of Rio Grande do Sul and Uruguay. The various regular artillery corps of the colonial army were reorganized as follows:

- The Artillery Regiment of Rio de Janeiro became the 1st Foot Artillery Corps
- The Artillery Battalion of Rio de Janeiro (*Henriques*) became the 2nd Foot Artillery Corps
- The Artillery Battalion of Santos became the 3rd Foot Artillery Corps
- The Artillery Battalion of Santa Catarina became the 4th Foot Artillery Corps

- The Artillery Battalion of Montevideo became the 5th Foot Artillery Corps
- The Artillery Corps of Espiritu Santu became the 6th Foot Artillery Corps
- The Artillery Corps of Bahia became the 7th Foot Artillery Corps
- The Artillery Corps of Pernambuco became the 8th Foot Artillery Corps
- The Artillery Corps of Piuaí became the 9th Foot Artillery Corps
- The Artillery Corps of Ceará became the 10th Foot Artillery Corps
- The Artillery Corps of Maranhão became the 11th Foot Artillery Corps
- The Artillery Corps of Pará became the 12th Foot Artillery Corps
- The Mounted Artillery Corps of the Court became the 1st Horse Artillery Corps
- The Mounted Artillery Corps of the Legion of São Paulo became the 2nd Horse Artillery Corps
- The Mounted Artillery Corps of São Pedro (Rio Grande do Sul) became the 3rd Horse Artillery Corps
- The Mounted Artillery Corps of Alagoas became the 4th Horse Artillery Corps
- The Mounted Artillery Corps of Paraiba became the 5th Horse Artillery Corps

Each foot artillery corps consisted of four companies/batteries, while a horse artillery corps corresponded to a single mounted company/battery. With the reorganization of December 1824 the units of the "Second Line" were re-structured in order to comprise 4 regiments of line infantry with two battalions each, 89 battalions of light infantry, 39 corps of cavalry (having different internal establishments) and a few corps of artillery. These units of the *Milicia* mostly continued to perform only auxiliary or police duties inside their home provinces.

Brazilian uniforms in 1824, from left to right: militia cavalry officer of the 2nd Line, musician of the line infantry, militia cavalry trooper of the 2nd Line from Diamantina and militia caçador of the 2nd Line from Rio de Janeiro.

The Regency Period and the Farrapos War, 1831–1845

Following the great political changes that were caused by Pedro I's abdication, the Brazilian Army had to be completely reorganized with the Imperial Decree of 4 May 1831. According to the latter the Brazilian regular forces were greatly reduced in their numbers and came to comprise the following units: 16 battalions of *Caçadores* with eight companies each, 5 regiments of cavalry with four squadrons each, 5 foot artillery corps with eight companies/batteries each and 1 horse artillery corps with four companies/batteries. The disbandment of several of the existing units caused a surplus of officers. This problem was resolved by creating a temporary corps, known as "Battalion of Officers-Soldiers", that was entirely made up of officers who did not have a commission. On 18 August 1831 all the military units of the "Second Line" and of the "Third Line" were disbanded, following the creation of the new National Guard.

The formation of the latter had been inspired by the liberal political ideas that were dominant during the Regency Period and thus it was to consist of all able-bodied Brazilians aged 21–60. The new corps was structured in independent infantry companies, which could serve only inside the borders of their home province. A single company was to comprise from a minimum of 50 men to a maximum of 140 men. Four companies could be assembled together to raise a battalion and the latter, once formed, could comprise two companies of *Caçadores*. The National Guard could comprise also units of cavalry, which would consist of companies having from a minimum of 70 to a maximum of 100 men. Two cavalry companies could be assembled together to create a squadron. Artillery units could be formed inside the National Guard only if specifically required by the central government. In 1834 the number of regular units was reduced again, since the infantry was now to consist of 8 *Caçadores* battalions and the cavalry of 4 regiments.

In 1839, following the great difficulties experienced in fighting against the Farrapos of Rio Grande do Sul, the Brazilian Army was re-structured to comprise the following units: 12 battalions of *Caçadores* with eight companies each, 3 regiments of cavalry with four squadrons each, 4 independent squadrons of cavalry with two companies each, 5 foot artillery battalions with eight companies/batteries each, 1 horse artillery corps with four companies/batteries, 4 companies of artificers and 2 mixed companies of *Pontonniers*/Sappers/Miners. For the first time the foot artillery was organized in battalions and a brand new corps of "technical troops" (*Pontonniers*/Sappers/Miners) was created. The latter, however, was extremely short-lived since it was impossible to recruit enough men capable of performing the duties required to the corps. Of the four companies of artificers two, already in existence as a single corps since 1809, were stationed in the Arsenal of

Uniforms of the Brazilian "Archers of the Imperial Guard" in 1815 (left) and in 1825 (right).

Brazilian officer (left) and trooper (right) of the Imperial Guard of Honour in 1831.

Rio de Janeiro while the remaining two (created in 1839) were garrisoned in Bahia and Pernambuco.

On 25 April 1842 the Brazilian Army was reorganized again, coming to comprise the following corps: 8 battalions of fusiliers with eight companies each, 8 battalions of *Caçadores* with six companies each, 3 regiments of cavalry with eight companies each, 4 battalions of foot artillery with eight companies/batteries each, 1 horse artillery corps with four companies/batteries and the Artificer Corps. It is important to note how this reorganization re-introduced line infantry units inside the Brazilian regular forces. The army of the Riograndense Republic, which caused so many troubles to the imperial forces, consisted almost entirely of gaucho cavalry plus some scarce infantry (performing only defensive duties) that was recruited from the inhabitans of the few Riograndense urban centres or from enemy deserters. The cavalry of the Farrapos was structured in regiments, which could have from a minimum of 400 men to a maximum of 800 men. These were assembled into companies of 50 gauchos each. The Riograndense cavalrymen were all armed as lancers and this gave them a great tactical advantage over their opponents who, at least initially, did not employ cavalry spears. Two of the Farrapos' mounted regiments (the number of which varied a lot during the period 1835–1845) were considered to be elite units. The 1st Corps of Lancers and the 2nd Corps of Lancers were collectively known as "*Lanceiros Negros*" since their members were all free blacks or mulattoes. Many of the latter had been freed by the Riograndense republican authorities and thus fought to protect their personal freedom.

From the Platine War to the Paraguayan War, 1846–1865

In 1846, with the gauchos of the Riograndese Republic who had benefitted from the general amnesty decreed during the previous year, a new regiment of cavalry was formed inside the Brazilian Army. In 1847 the Brazilian naval artillery was completely reorganized, since it was transformed into a naval infantry corps known as "Corps of Naval Fusiliers". This consisted of ten companies of marines. The original officers of the corps were absorbed into the foot artillery of the army – which needed competent commanders – and were replaced by new ones. Following the end of the conflict fought during 1848–1849 between Denmark and the German Duchy of Schleswig-Holstein, the Brazilian authorities decided to recruit a contingent of mercenaries from the experienced soldiers of the recently-disbanded Schleswig-Holstein Army. The audacious recruiting operation worked well and led to the formation, in 1851, of two German units with a total of 1,000 mercenaries. These comprised one battalion of *Caçadores* (equipped with Dreyse needle guns) and one corps of horse artillery. The German light infantrymen participated in the Battle of Caseros in 1852 with distinction. Despite this their battalion, together

Uniforms of the Brazilian National Guard in 1831, from left to right: infantrymen, infantry officer and cavalryman.

with the German horse artillery corps, was disbanded soon after the end of the Platine War.

Meanwhile, in 1851, the whole Brazilian Army had been re-structured to comprise the following units: 8 battalions of fusiliers with eight companies each (numbered 1-8), 7 battalions of *Caçadores* with six companies each (numbered 9-15), 4 regiments of cavalry with eight companies each, 4 battalions of foot artillery with eight companies/batteries each, 1 horse artillery corps with four companies/batteries and the Artificer Corps. In 1852 one battalion of fusiliers was disbanded and a new regiment of cavalry was formed in Rio Grande do Sul. The following units of the Brazilian Army participated in the Platine War, being part of Urquiza "*Ejército Grande*":

- 5th Fusilier Battalion
- 6th Fusilier Battalion
- 7th Fusilier Battalion
- 8th Fusilier Battalion
- 11th *Caçadores* Battalion
- 13th *Caçadores* Battalion
- 2nd Cavalry Regiment
- Horse Artillery Corps

In 1852 the Corps of Naval Fusiliers received its new denomination of "Naval Battalion" and started to consist of eight companies: six of naval fusiliers and two of naval artillerymen. This new internal organization remained unchanged for several decades. During 1855 an Engineer Battalion was created, which consisted of four companies. On 19 September 1850 the National Guard, which had not performed particularly well during the Farrapos War, was reorganized. It was now to consist of two distinct branches, the Active National Guard and the Reserve National Guard. The first would consist of all the able-bodied Brazilian citizens aged 21–50 and could be deployed to perform combat duties. The second would consist of all the able-bodied individuals over 50 years of age and could be deployed only to perform static defensive duties. The basic unit of the National Guard remained the company, which could comprise from a minimum of 80 men to a maximum of 150. Battalions could be formed by assembling together a minimum of four companies to a maximum of eight. Two companies of *Caçadores* could be included in each foot battalion. The National Guard cavalry was structured in companies with 70–100 men, two mounted companies made up a squadron. As previously, artillery units could be formed inside the National Guard only if specifically required by the central government.

With the creation of the National Guard in 1831 the military units of the "Second Line" were officially disbanded. Very soon, however, the various provinces of Brazil started to feel the need for some locally-recruited regular corps that could act as a sort of gendarmerie and as garrison troops. For this reason a new category of provincial regular units appeared, the so-called "Fixed Corps". These had many different official denominations, which varied from province to province: "*Pedestres*", "*Ligeiros*" and "*Caçadores da Montanha*" were the most popular ones. Despite being part, at least on paper, of the regular army, the Fixed Corps were administered in an autonomous way by the various provincial governments and were usually much more effective than the National Guard. In 1865 they were all disbanded following the outbreak of the Paraguayan War and their members were used to form new units for the regular army. The latter, in 1864, consisted of the following corps: 7 battalions of fusiliers with eight companies each, 7 battalions of *Caçadores* with six companies each, 5 regiments of cavalry with four squadrons each (one equipped with carbines and three with lances), 4 battalions of foot artillery with eight companies/batteries each, 1 horse artillery corps with four companies/batteries, 1 engineer battalion with four companies and 1 corps of artificers. The Brazilian expeditionary force that took part in the Uruguayan War consisted of the following units:

- 3rd Fusilier Battalion
- 4th Fusilier Battalion
- 6th Fusilier Battalion
- 13th *Caçadores* Battalion
- 2nd Regiment of Cavalry
- 3rd Regiment of Cavalry
- 4th Regiment of Cavalry
- 5th Regiment of Cavalry
- Horse Artillery Corps
- 6 provisional corps of National Guard cavalry from Rio Grande do Sul (gauchos)
- 1 brigade of volunteer cavalry from Rio Grande do Sul (gauchos)

After the outbreak of the Paraguayan War, the Brazilian generals quickly realized that the small regular forces under their command were far from enough to beat back the well trained Paraguayan soldiers. As a first measure to face the emergency, all the "Fixed" corps (garrison units) were transferred to the southern provinces, to hold the breach until the regular forces could be fully mobilized. Obviously, this was not enough, as in 1866, with the arrival of the new recruits, the Brazilian Army was expanded and partly reorganized. All the "Fixed" corps were disbanded and incorporated into the regular forces. They provided much of the manpower for the expansion of the army, with their soldiers being used as cadres for the new units, or were simply broken up and used as reinforcements. Eight more infantry battalions were formed, all of "*Caçadores*", for a total

Brazilian uniforms of the Regency Period, from left to right: caçador, officer of the Battalion of Officers-Soldiers, officer of Rio de Janeiro's National Guard infantry and fusilier in campaign dress.

The uniforms of the Brazilian fusiliers according to the 1845 dress regulations, from left to right: officers, private and musician.

of 22. The 4th and 5th Cavalry Regiments were broken up and used as cadres to form five new corps of "*Caçadores a Cavallo*" ("Mounted Rifles"), each having 638 men in 4 squadrons. A 5th Battalion of Foot Artillery was raised and the Horse Artillery Corps had to provide a cadre for the formation of a second Provisional Corps. The Battalion of Engineers remained basically unchanged, but at a higher establishment. Since 1865, one squadron of Train had been added to the technical units.

The Brazilian National Guard had been completely reorganized in 1851, in order to increase the quality of its troops. It provided the reserves for the regular army and was made up of volunteers from a multitude of units across the whole country, which were to be recruited, organized and administered by the individual provinces. The Imperial Court also raised its own National Guard units from the country at large, as if it was a province in its own right. These units, known as "of the Court", were better trained and equipped than ordinary provincial units and served as a model for the "*Guardia Nacional*" corps as a whole. The units "of the Court" had a certain number of well-to-do gentlemen in their ranks, while most national guardsmen from the provinces were simply patriotic but ordinary men. The National Guard comprised units from all the branches of service (infantry, cavalry and artillery) but no separate light infantry ones, because each infantry battalion could have two companies of "*Caçadores*".

In 1865, Imperial Decree No. 3,383 mobilized 14,796 "*Guardias Nacionales*" for war service. Some were sent to join the regular army in the field, others to perform "police" functions behind the lines or to relieve regular troops in provincial garrisons. The National Guard continued to recruit throughout the war, as the demand for new units for all sorts of duties continued to grow. Unfortunately, there are no available figures for how many national guardsmen were eventually mobilized during the conflict (presumably well over 100,000 men). We know that the province of Rio Grande do Sul alone mobilized a total of 43,500 soldiers of the National Guard, of whom 29,200 saw combat. Equally, there is no complete listing of the number of units raised. This is not very surprising, considering that the conflict saw a continual process of units being raised, disbanded, amalgamated and renumbered, to the point that even following the history of a single unit can be very difficult. For example, there were many units designated as "Provisional Corps", which were considered to be part of the National Guard. Evidence suggests that these were "ad hoc" units, formed with drafts from various sources and provisionally attached to the regular army. Although the Empire had a large National Guard, Brazilian law stated that its individual provincial units could only be used beyond the national borders when their respective home provinces were attacked by outside forces. The Paraguayan attacks against Mato Grosso and Rio Grande do Sul therefore meant that only these two provinces could send National Guard units to assist the regular army in the field. Brazilian public opinion was incensed at the "outrages" of Paraguay, whose soldiers had invaded Brazil's border provinces. National cohesion was soon achieved and public support for the war was overwhelming. It was time for Brazil to call on its large population to defend the nation, so the Brazilian government opted for the creation of a whole new class of volunteer troops, organized separately from the National Guard and to exist for the duration of the war with Paraguay. With the Decree No. 3,371 of 7 January 1865, the Emperor ordered the formation of the new "*Corpo de Voluntários da Pátria*" or "CVP". The response to this new force was very enthusiastic and thousands of men from all over the country answered the call within a short time and signed up. The new infantry battalions of the "CVP" were soon formed, with the 1st, 2nd, 4th and 9th being raised by the Imperial Court. They played a prominent role during the years of war 1865–1870, since they made up the bulk of the Brazilian Army's infantry forces.

Uniforms and weapons

In 1822 the Brazilian military forces of Pedro I were still uniformed according to the dress regulations that had been promulgated for Portuguese Brazil in 1816. The Prince Regent, in fact, did not order the compilation of a new "plan of uniforms" but simply ordered all his soldiers to wear a peculiar badge on the left shoulder in order to be easily distinguishable from the Portuguese metropolitan soldiers deployed in Brazil. The badge, worn until 1825, consisted of a green disk and a yellow chevron bearing the inscription "*INDEPENDENCIA OU MORTE*" ("Independence or Death"). For the M1816 uniforms worn by the early Brazilian military forces, see the relevant pictures and captions. In 1823 the first official dress regulations of the Brazilian Army were promulgated. These, however, did not change the existing uniforms in a significant way except for the introduction of new "national" distinctions (like the cockade). Only the *Caçadores* received a brand new uniform with the 1823 regulations. The elite "Battalion of the Emperor", existing until 1831, was not uniformed like the other grenadier units of the Brazilian Army. It had black bearskin headdress with red plume and white cords-and-flounders, dark blue coat with red cuffs piped in white and red epaulettes, white frontal lapels, white cuff flaps, dark blue collar, red turnbacks and white trousers. For the uniform of the Imperial Guard of Honour, see the relevant pictures and captions.

The uniforms of the Brazilian Army according to the 1845 dress regulations, from left to right: foot artilleryman, sapper of the fusiliers, fusilier, officer of the fusiliers in campaign dress and officer of the fusiliers in parade dress.

The uniforms of the Brazilian Army according to the 1845 dress regulations, from left to right: officer of the artificers, sergeant of the fusiliers in campaign dress, private of a depot fusilier company and caçador.

Uniforms of the Brazilian caçadores according to the 1845 dress regulations, from left to right: officers in parade dress and officer in stable dress.

Uniforms of the Brazilian caçadores according to the 1845 dress regulations: private in parade dress (left) and private in stable dress (right).

The four infantry battalions of the "Corps of Foreigners" were dressed quite similarly to the Brazilian "national" units; see the relevant pictures and captions for more details. The lancers, instead, were uniformed with an elegant Polish-style dress having facings in the Brazilian national colours of green and yellow. The military units of the 2nd Line were uniformed similarly to the regular ones, except for the corps of "*Henriques*" (free blacks). These were dressed, since the 18th century, with white uniforms having red facings. With the creation of the National Guard in 1831, the various units of "*Henriques*" disappeared.

During the Regency Period the uniforms of the Brazilian Army changed very little, since no new dress regulations were promulgated. With the new organization introduced in 1831 the line infantry was disbanded and thus a new uniform was introduced for the *Caçadores*. This, for the first time entirely dark green, is reproduced in one of the pictures. The latter also shows the appearance of the short-lived "Battalion of Officers-Soldiers". For the uniforms of the newly-created National Guard prescribed by the 1831 dress regulations, see the relevant pictures and captions. In 1842 the line infantry was re-formed and was given new dark blue uniforms, which were very similar to those adopted with the new dress regulations of 1845. They comprised a tall "*bonnet de police*" fatigue cap that was worn with campaign dress and became extremely popular (see the relevant pictures and captions). The military forces of the secessionist Riograndense Republic had no uniforms to speak of, except for the two elite "Corps of Lancers" that were made up of black or mulatto soldiers. These wore a red gaucho-style dress, with red "bag" cap and blouse. The cockade appointed on the chest and the pennon of the lance were in the colours of Rio Grande do Sul (green, red and yellow). The 1845 dress regulations gave a distinctive "British" appearance to the Brazilian Army, with the introduction of a double-breasted coat; see the relevant pictures for more details. The foot artillery was dressed as follows: red conical shako (different from that of the infantry battalions) having black pompom and falling plume, brass front plate and black cord wrapped around the main body; dark blue double-breasted coat with red collar and pointed cuffs, dark blue epaulettes with yellow crescents and red fringes, red turnbacks, dark blue cuff flaps with red piping, dark blue trousers with red side-stripe and white belt equipment. The artificers were dressed similarly to the horse artillery but with black collar and cuffs piped in red.

The 1852 dress regulations marked a real "revolution" for the uniforms of the Brazilian Army, since they introduced a single-breasted coat for parade dress and a single-breasted tunic for service dress. See the relevant pictures and captions for more details. On campaign, the *Caçadores* used a uniform with visorless cap and jacket (these were dark blue for the line infantry). The few sappers attached to the staff of each line infantry battalion wore a peculiar uniform comprising a black "busby" with white plume and red "side bag", long apron made of jaguar skin on the chest and of buff leather under the waistbelt. The German mercenaries of 1851–1852 were dressed with their Schleswig-Holstein uniforms, including Prussian "spiked helmet", but with Brazilian cockade. The Engineer Battalion created in 1855 only had the single-breasted tunic for service dress. The new dress regulations of 1858, which remained valid until 1866, slightly modified the existing uniforms by simply altering the dimensions of some elements. With the M1852 and M1858 uniforms the artificers continued to be dressed like the horse artillery but with black facings. The uniforms for the National Guard prescribed by the 1831 dress regulations were frequently altered by the various provincial governments. In Rio de Janeiro Province, for example, during the 1840s the members of the National Guard wore a black cap resembling a Polish "*czapka*" together with a dark blue coat having facings in different colours. The cavalry officers had a flamboyant hussar-style uniform, which was red for the 1st Regiment and dark blue for the 2nd Regiment. The new dress regulations for the National Guard of 1851 restored order. For more details about them, see the relevant pictures and captions. The uniforms of the so-called "Fixed Corps" were defined by the single provincial governments. They, however, followed the patterns of the regulars' dress quite closely. During the whole period 1825–1865 the Brazilian naval artillery/marines were always dressed like the line infantry, in dark blue with red facings.

For long time the musket used by all the Brazilian foot units was the ubiquitous Brown Bess, which remained the standard infantry weapon of the Brazilian Army until 1857. During the latter year all the Brazilian foot troops were re-equipped with new percussion muskets, all Belgian-made Minié ones. In 1858 a certain number of similar Enfield weapons were bought from England. By 1864 the line infantry muskets were either Belgian "*Espingardas Minié*" or Pattern 1853 Enfields. The "*Caçadores*" battalions were armed with the same weapons as the line infantry, but in their light infantry short version. The muskets of the "*Fusileiros*" had triangular socket bayonets, while the carbines of the "*Caçadores*" had sword-bayonets (of the "yataghan" type for Enfield carbines). At the beginning of the Para-

Uniforms of the Brazilian mounted troops according to the 1845 dress regulations, from left to right: horse artilleryman, cavalryman in campaign dress, cavalry officer and cavalryman in parade dress.

guayan War a decision was made to use only 14.8 mm balls, in order to avoid any confusion regarding supply of ammunition. For this reason, all the Enfields of the Brazilian Army (whose caliber was 14.66 mm) were returned to the army's arsenal to be re-rifled to the correct size.

In 1852 the Brazilian government had bought 900 Dreyse M1841 needle-guns for the war against Rosas. In 1866 an independent company of "*Caçadores*" was formed to test these weapons on the Paraguayan fields of battle. In December of the same year the Prussian-born Lieutenant Meyer was selected to command it, because he already had experience with the needle-gun. Gradually the company grew in numbers and was attached to the 15th Battalion of "*Caçadores*". The whole battalion was later completely re-equipped with the Prussian Dreyse but this jammed on many occasions. Apparently, climatic conditions in Paraguay were not ideal for this kind of weapon. As a result, the Brazilian tests with the new rifle were suspended. By 1865 the majority of the Brazilian officers were armed with Colt or Lefaucheux revolvers but percussion pistols were still in use, being either Minié (most of which were smoothbores) or Enfield ones. The Brazilian cavalry was armed with Minié or Enfield carbines, which had replaced the previous Brown Bess flintlock ones. The Brazilian cavalrymen were also equipped with sabers model 1831 or model 1851, which were Brazilian copies of the excellent French 1822 light cavalry saber. These were used in two different versions, one for officers and one for soldiers. A certain number of old British Pattern 1796 light cavalry sabers were still carried, despite being officially out of use since 1831. Cavalry also had lances, which were of the 1844 model (imported from England) or of the 1864 model (imported from France). The Rio Grande do Sul National Guard cavalry was armed with the cross-type lances and "*bolas*" of the gauchos.

Uniforms of the Brazilian National Guard in 1840, from left to right: senior officer, infantry sergeant and drum-major.

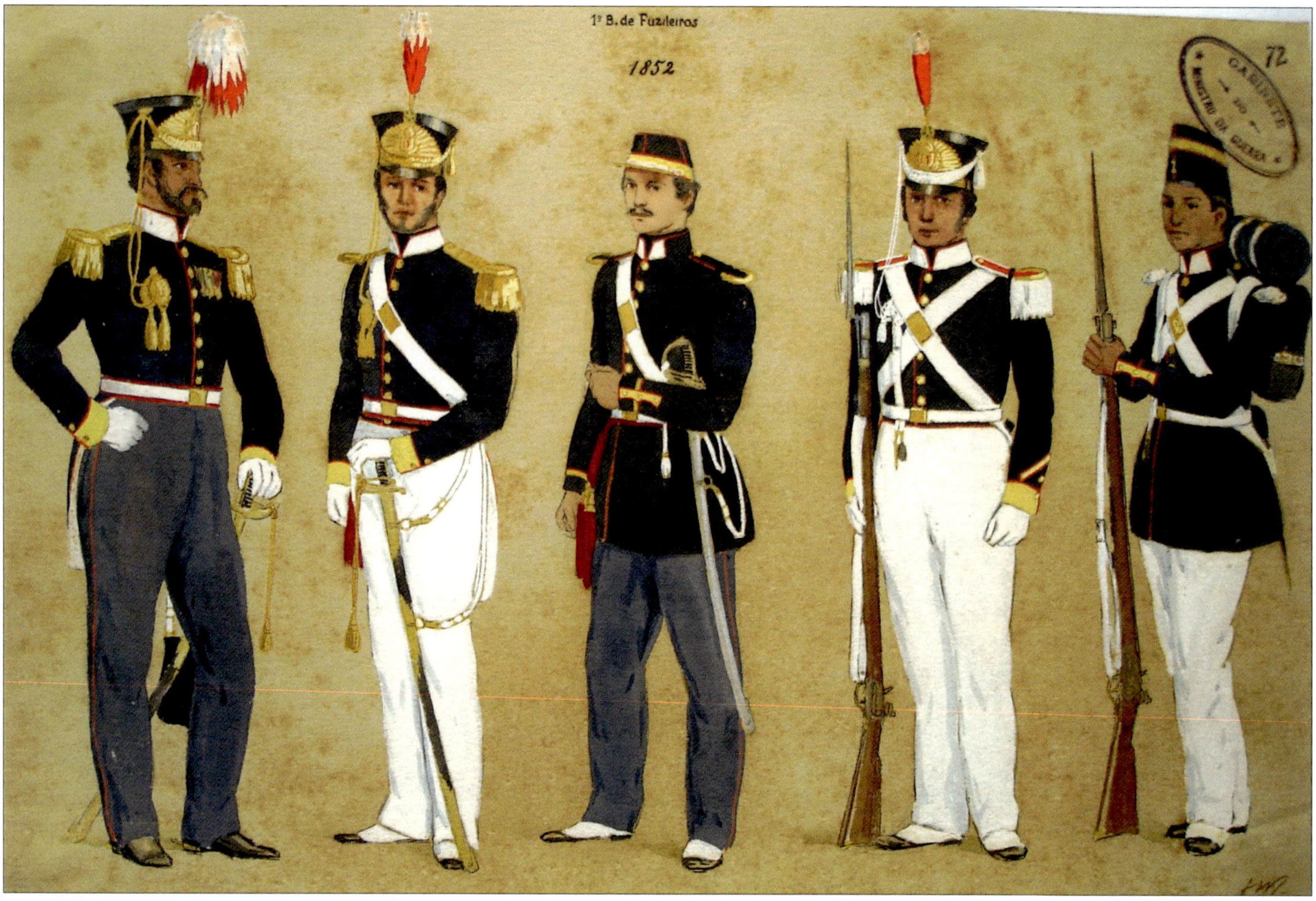
1º B. de Fuzileiros
1852
72

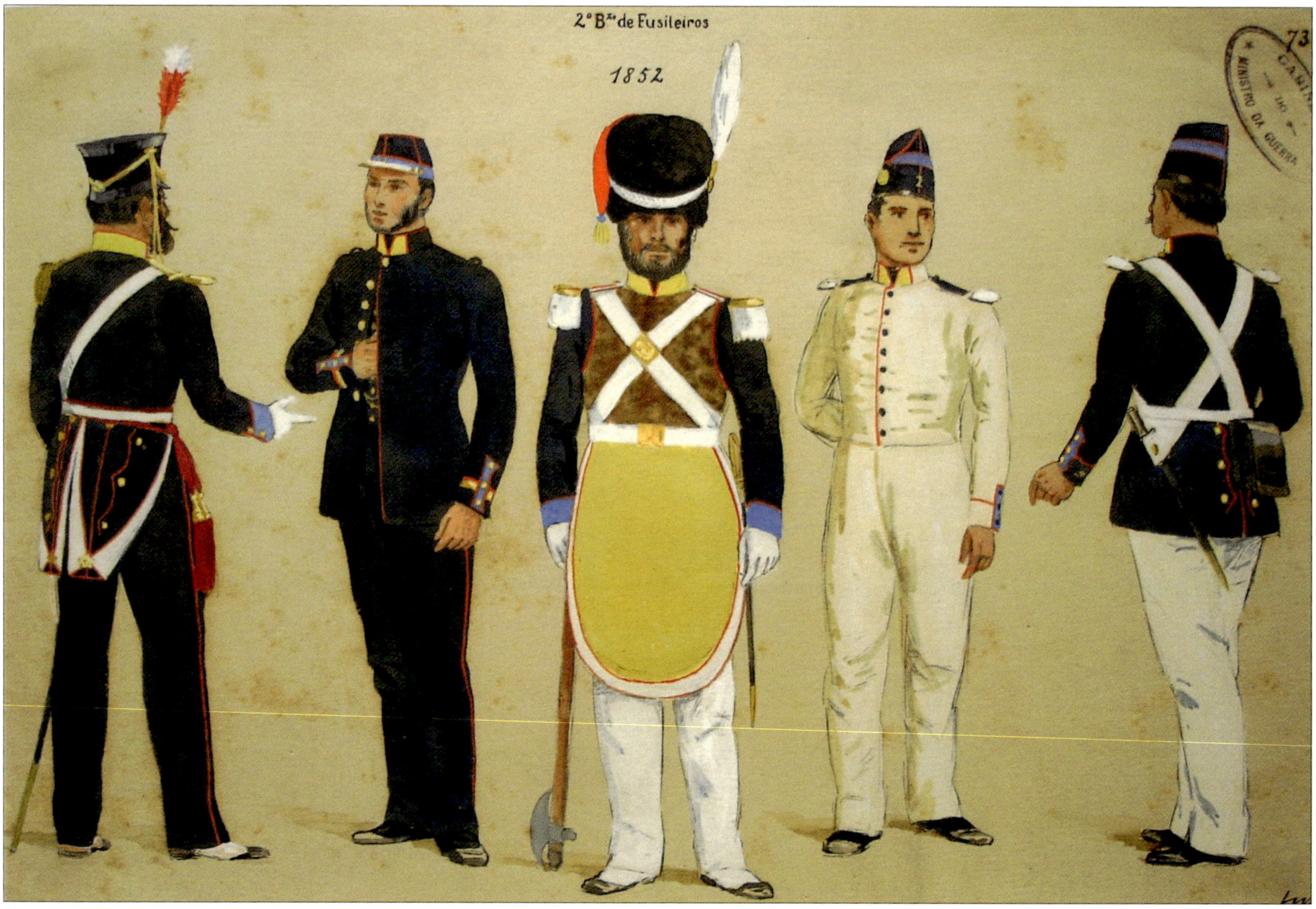
2º Bºⁿ de Fusileiros
1852
73

Uniforms of the Brazilian caçadores according to the 1852 dress regulations, from left to right: officer in parade dress, officer in campaign dress, officer in parade dress, private in parade dress and private in campaign dress.

Opposite page, above: Uniforms of the Brazilian fusiliers according to the 1852 dress regulations, from left to right: officers in parade dress, officer in campaign dress, private in parade dress and private in campaign dress.

Opposite page, below: Uniforms of the Brazilian fusiliers according to the 1852 dress regulations, from left to right: officer in parade dress, officer in campaign dress, sapper, private in fatigue dress and private in campaign dress.

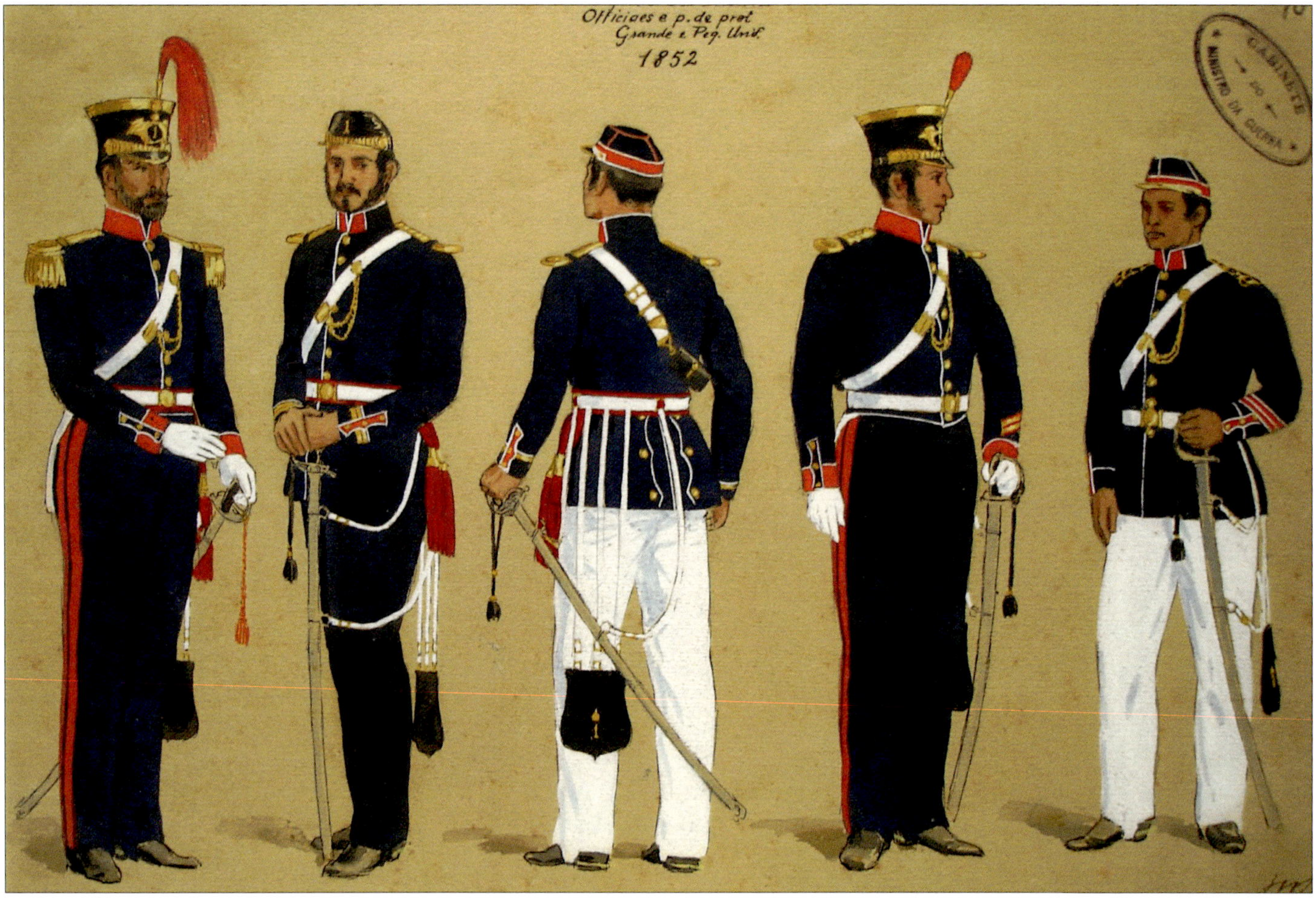

Officiaes e p. de pret
Grande e Peq. Unif.
1852

4º Reg.to de Cavallaria
1852

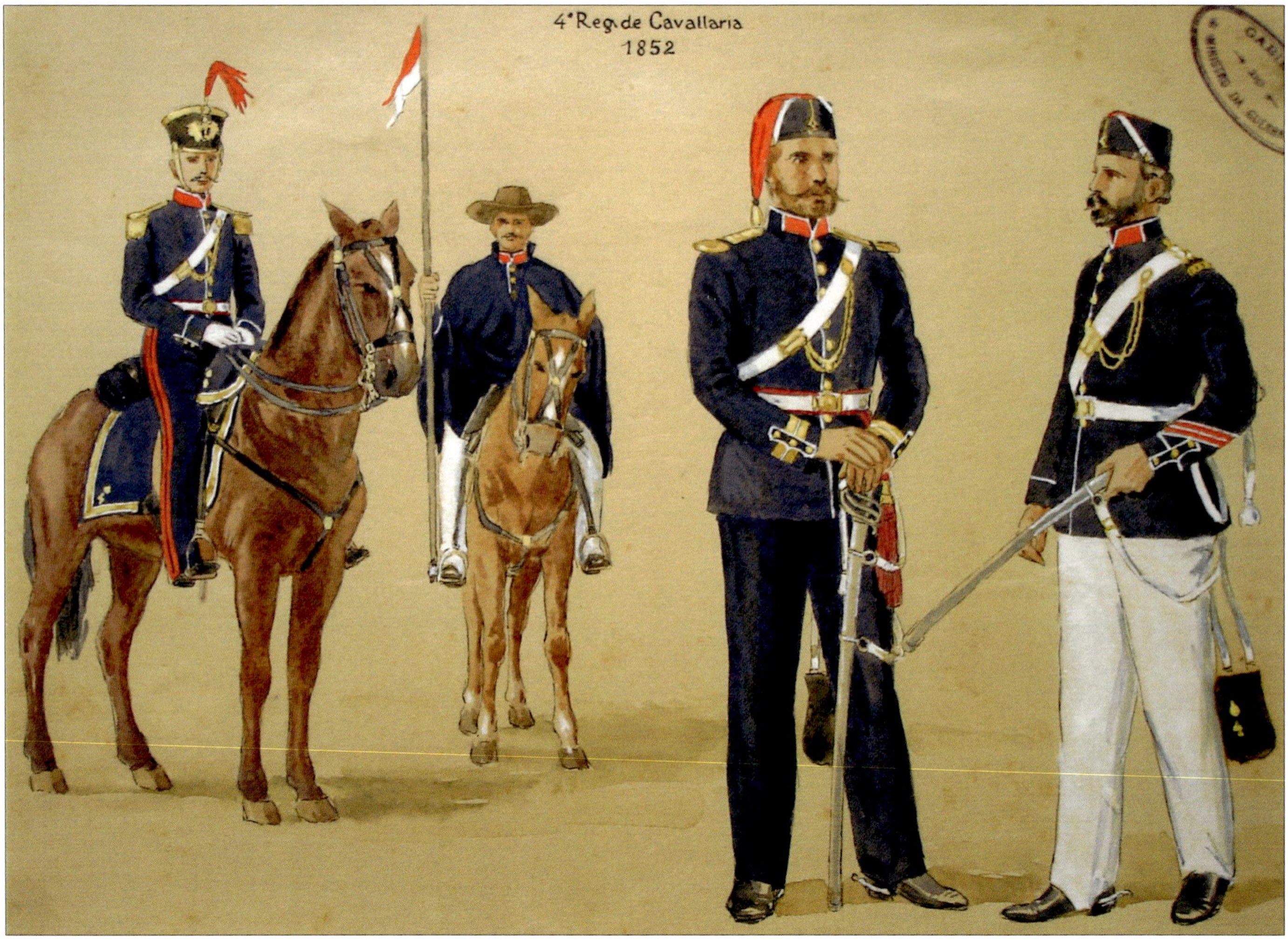

Uniforms of the Brazilian 1st Foot Artillery Battalion according to the 1852 dress regulations, from left to right: officers in parade dress, officer in campaign dress, gunner in parade dress and gunner in campaign dress.

Opposite page, above: Uniforms of the Brazilian cavalry according to the 1852 dress regulations, from left to right: officer in parade dress, officers in campaign dress, NCO in parade dress and NCO in campaign dress.

Opposite page, below: Uniforms of the Brazilian cavalry according to the 1852 dress regulations, from left to right: officer in parade dress, trooper in campaign dress, officer in campaign dress and NCO in campaign dress.

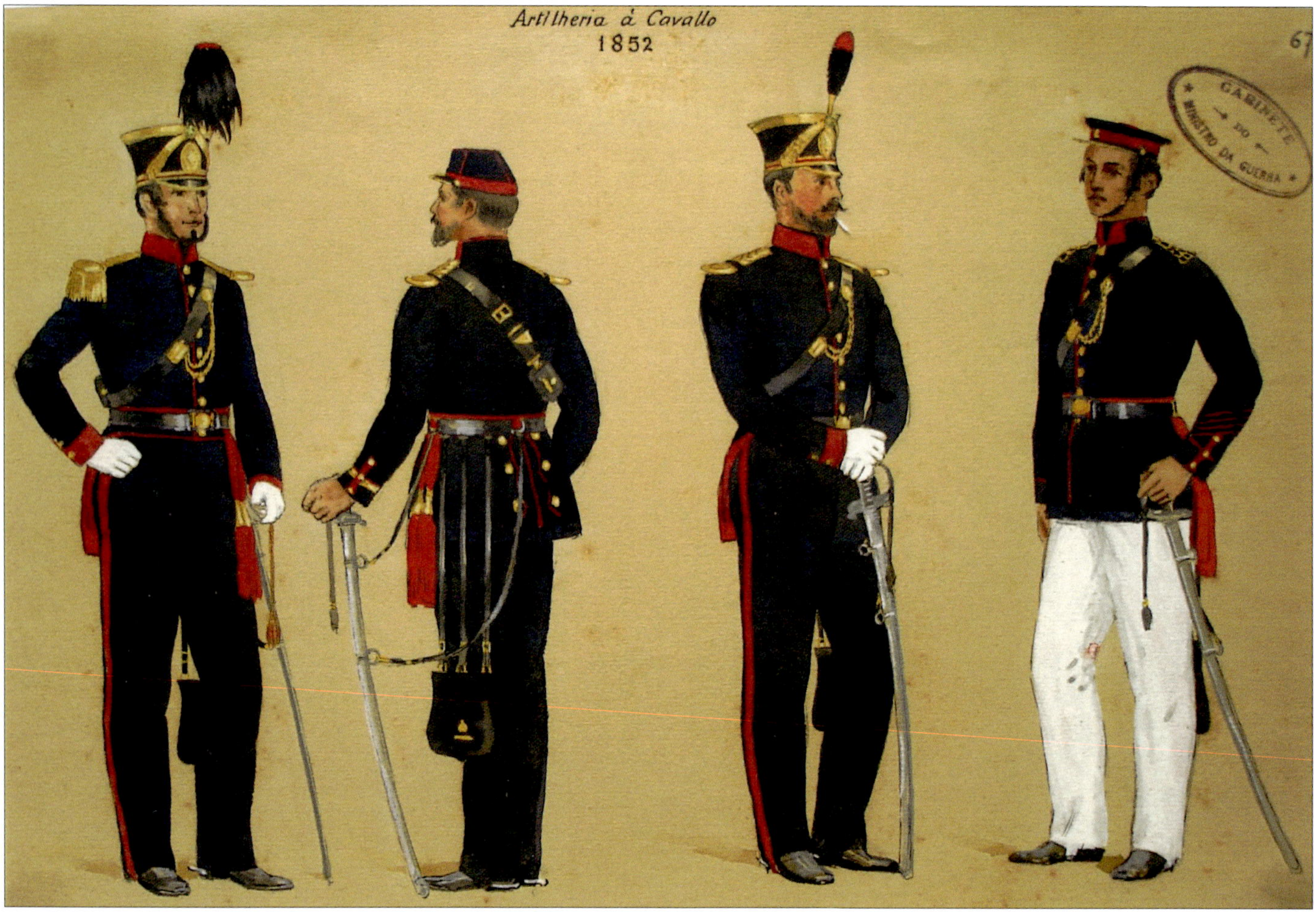

Artilheria à Cavallo
1852
67
GABINETE DO MINISTRO DA GUERRA

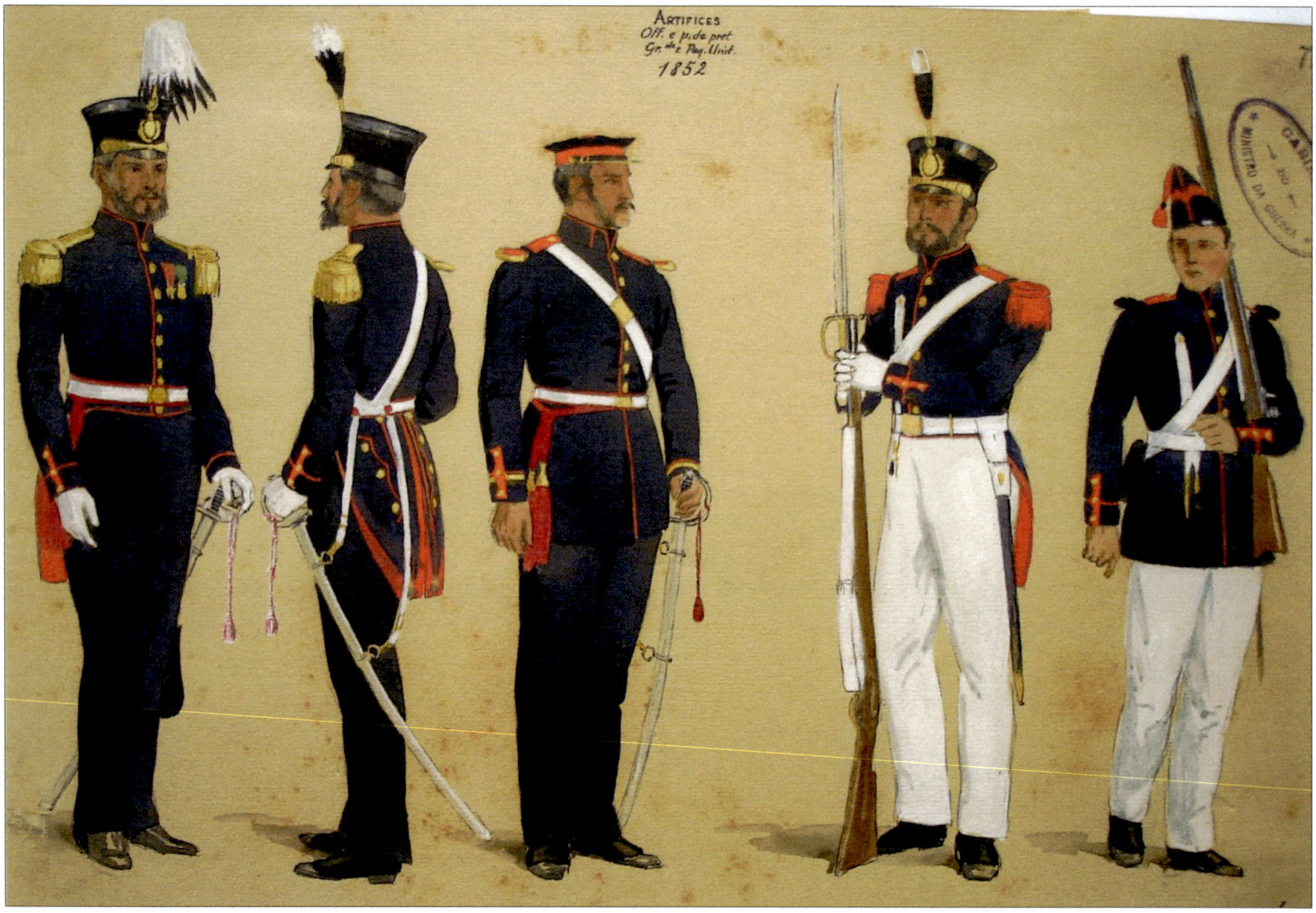

Artifices
Off. e p. de pret
Gr.de e Peq. Unif.
1852

Uniforms of the Brazilian National Guard in 1851, from left to right: artillery officer, fusilier officer and fusilier.

Opposite page, above: Uniforms of the Brazilian horse artillery according to the 1852 dress regulations, from left to right: officer in parade dress, trooper in campaign dress, trooper in campaign dress and trooper in stable dress.

Opposite page, below: Uniforms of the Brazilian artificers according to the 1852 dress regulations, from left to right: officers in parade dress, officer in campaign dress, private in parade dress and private in campaign dress.

Uniforms of the Brazilian National Guard in 1851, from left to right: caçador officer in parade dress, caçador in parade dress, caçador officer in campaign dress and caçador in stable dress.

Uniforms of the Brazilian National Guard in 1851, from left to right: superior officer, officer of Rio de Janeiro 1st National Guard Cavalry Regiment in parade dress, officer of Rio de Janeiro 2nd National Guard Cavalry Regiment in campaign dress and trooper of Rio de Janeiro 2nd National Guard Cavalry Regiment in parade dress.

Uniforms of the Brazilian Engineer Battalion in 1855: private (left) and NCO (right).

Uniforms of the Brazilian fusiliers according to the 1858 dress regulations, from left to right: officer in parade dress, officer in campaign dress, private in parade dress and private in campaign dress.

Uniforms of the Brazilian fusiliers according to the 1858 dress regulations, from left to right: sapper, musician, drummer and drum-major.

Uniforms of the Brazilian caçadores according to the 1858 dress regulations, from left to right: officer in parade dress, officer in campaign dress, private in parade dress and private in campaign dress.

Uniforms of the Brazilian cavalry according to the 1858 dress regulations, from left to right: officer in parade dress, trooper in parade dress, NCO in campaign dress and trumpeter.

Uniforms of the Brazilian foot artillery according to the 1858 dress regulations, from left to right: officers in parade dress, gunners in campaign dress and musician.

41

Uniforms of the Brazilian horse artillery according to the 1858 dress regulations, from left to right: officer in parade dress, officer in campaign dress, trumpeter in parade dress and trumpeter in campaign dress.

Uniforms of the Brazilian artificers according to the 1858 dress regulations, from left to right: officer in parade dress, officer in campaign dress and private in campaign dress.

Brazilian National Guard "of the Court" in 1858, from left to right: cavalryman, sapper and infantryman.

The Argentine Army

History and organization

In 1820 the military forces of the Argentine Republic were completely reorganized, after many years spent fighting against the Spanish troops in present-day Bolivia and in Uruguay. They came to comprise the following corps: Fixed Infantry Battalion of Buenos Aires (with six companies), Patrician Legion (a regiment with three battalions recruited from the merchants and craftsmen of Buenos Aires), Infantry Regiment "*del Orden*" (with six companies), Dragoon Regiment "*del Orden*" (with four squadrons), Hussar Regiment of Buenos Aires (with two squadrons), Hussar Regiment "*del Orden*" (with two squadrons) and Artillery Battalion of Buenos Aires (with six companies). During the years 1820–1824 some new units were created: Cazadores Battalion (with six companies, like the Fixed Infantry Battalion of Buenos Aires that was re-named "Fusilier Battalion"), Patrician Infantry Brigade (formed by assembling together the Patrician Legion and the Infantry Regiment "*del Orden*"), Blandengues Cavalry Regiment (the former Hussar Regiment "*del Orden*"), 1st Patrician Cavalry Regiment of Buenos Aires (with two squadrons), 2nd Patrician Cavalry Regiment of Buenos Aires (with two squadrons), Cuirassier Regiment of Buenos Aires and Hussar Squadron of Entre Ríos. Some of these corps were the direct heirs of glorious military traditions that had emerged during the early years of the 19th century. The "*Patricio*" or "Patrician" units, for example, took their name from the famous infantry corps of Buenos Aires' militia that was created on 13 September 1806 to fight against the British military forces that attempted to invade the River Plate. The "*Patricios*" were a symbol of Buenos Aires and are still considered today as the oldest unit of the Argentine Army. The *Blandengues* were formed as a Spanish colonial cavalry corps as early as 1752. The word "*Blandengues*" means "those who brandish" and thus was used, in the Viceroyalty of La Plata, to identify those cavalry soldiers who were equipped with the peculiar long spear of the gauchos. The *Blandengues* were organized as a corps of light cavalry, which was tasked with defending the borders of Buenos Aires Province from the frequent incursions of the natives living in the "*pampa*". The *Blandengues* used the same methods of guerrilla warfare that were employed by their opponents and had special personal equipment, including some distinctive "gaucho" elements (boots, spurs and saddles). The "Frontier Corps of the *Blandengues* of Buenos Aires" was officially organized in 1780 on the basis of three independent

Uniforms of the Argentine infantry during the Cisplatine War: officer (left) and private (right).
Colour plate by Louis de Beaufort, part of the ASKB Military Collection.

frontier cavalry companies of the militia that had existed since 1752. All the military units existing during 1820–1824, except for the Hussar Squadron of Entre Ríos, were mostly recruited from Buenos Aires Province. As a result, the military contribution of the interior provinces to the formation of the central Argentine Army was extremely limited. Argentina, in addition to the regular forces described above, also had a militia. This was divided into two main branches, according to a law promulgated on 17 December 1823: the "*Milicia Activa*" or "Active Militia" that comprised all the able-bodied men aged 17–45 and the "*Milicia Pasiva*" or "Passive Militia" that comprised all the able-bodied men aged 45–60. The first could perform auxiliary duties for the army, the second could perform only static defensive duties. The Active Militia of Buenos Aires Province was the only one having a good degree of discipline. It consisted of one infantry regiment with three battalions (having six companies each), four cavalry regiments with four squadrons each and one company of artillery.

The Cisplatine War

With the outbreak of the war with the Empire of Brazil in 1825, Argentina had to re-structure her military forces very rapidly in order to have a sufficient number of regular units to fight in Uruguay. The whole Argentine Army was reorganized to comprise the following corps, according to the law of 31 May 1825: 4 infantry battalions with six companies each (increased to 5 in 1826), 6 cavalry regiments with four squadrons each (increased to 12 in 1826) and 1 artillery battalion with six companies/batteries. All the Argentine provinces would contribute to the formation of the new units. The infantry battalions consisted of four fusilier companies, one company of grenadiers and one company of *cazadores* (light infantry). Most of the new units of the Argentine Army were created from zero, while other were created from existing corps: the 1st Infantry Battalion was the former *Cazadores* Battalion, the 4th Infantry Battalion was the former Fusilier Battalion, the 1st Cavalry Regiment was formed by assembling together the two Patrician Cavalry Regiments of Buenos Aires, the 5th Cavalry Regiment was the former Hussar Regiment of Buenos Aires, the 6th Cavalry Regiment was the former *Blandengues* Cavalry Regiment, the 7th Cavalry Regiment was the former Cuirassier Regiment of Buenos Aires. The 4th Cavalry Regiment, organized and commanded by Juan Lavalle, was a heavy unit having full cuirassier equipment. The last three cavalry regiments to be formed were numbered 16–18, since the planned units numbered 10–15 never came into existence. The 16th Cavalry Regiment was created by José de Olavarría, a veteran of the Wars of Independence who had been the commander of the "Hussars of Junín" (the most important cavalry unit of the Peruvian Army). It was a lancer corps uniformed with elegant hussar-style uniforms in green. The 17th Cavalry Regiment was created by assembling together the surviving veterans of the glorious "Mounted Grenadiers Regiment", who had just returned from Peru after having fought for a long time against the Spaniards. The Mounted Grenadiers Regiment was created on 16 March 1812 by José de San Martín, the "*libertador*" of Argentina, and took part in all the most important campaigns fought by Argentina during the Wars of Independence. It is still considered today as the senior mounted unit of the Argentine Army. In April 1826 the surviving veterans of the corps were reorganized as

Argentine line cavalryman of the Cisplatine War. *Colour plate by Louis de Beaufort, part of the ASKB Military Collection.*

Argentine line cavalryman, with cuirass, of the Cisplatine War. *Colour plate by Louis de Beaufort, part of the ASKB Military Collection.*

a single squadron, acting as the mounted escort of the Argentine president, later they were transformed into the new 17th Cavalry Regiment. In addition to the units listed above, the Argentine cavalry of the Cisplatine War also comprised another four corps, namely the Cavalry Regiment "Hussars Defenders of the National Honour", created in 1826 to remain as garrison in Buenos Aires, the "*Colorados de las Conchas*", a cavalry unit that had been raised in 1812 as part of Buenos Aires' militia, the "Cuirassiers of the Guard", a single squadron later expanded to become a regiment and the "German Lancers", a single cavalry squadron recruited from German emigrants living in Argentina (following the Brazilian example). Attached to the 1st Company of the Artillery Battalion there was a Company of Sappers. In 1826 a new "Regiment of Light Artillery" (mounted) was created, consisting of two squadrons with two companies/batteries each. It is interesting to note that two units of the Argentine Army were entirely made up of Uruguayans: the 3rd Infantry Battalion, which was formed by converting the "*Libertos Orientales*" Battalion (a corps of free black Uruguayan patriots) and later became the nucleus of the new Uruguayan Army as the 1st Infantry Battalion or Florida Battalion and the 9th Cavalry Regiment, which was formed by converting the "*Dragones Orientales*" Regiment, a cavalry corps of Uruguayan patriots commanded by Manuel Oribe.

The military forces of Rosas, 1829–1835

On 1 October 1829, after the demobilization that followed the end of the Cisplatine War, the Argentine Army was greatly reduced in its numbers and came to comprise the following units: 2 battalions of infantry, 2 regiments of cavalry and 1 battalion of artillery. The two foot units were the former 1st Infantry Battalion and 4th Infantry Battalion. The first, renamed "*Cazadores* Battalion of the River Plate", consisted of six companies (four centre ones, one of heavy infantry and one of light infantry) and was quite short-lived since it was disbanded in 1833. The second, renamed "Argentine Guard Battalion", had the same internal composition but included also a small detachment of sappers. On 9 January 1831 the old Patrician Legion of Buenos Aires was reorganized as the "*Patricios* Regiment", consisting of three battalions with six

Left: Argentine officer of the "*Colorados de las Conchas*" Regiment, Cisplatine War. *Colour plate by Louis de Beaufort, part of the ASKB Military Collection.*

Right: Argentine officer of the 17th Line Cavalry Regiment, Cisplatine War. *Colour plate by Louis de Beaufort, part of the ASKB Military Collection.*

infantry companies and one artillery company each. Despite having the status of a regular corps, the *Patricios* Regiment was a militia unit since all the able-bodied male inhabitants of the city of Buenos Aires aged 17–45 were required to serve in it. On 15 February 1840 the *Patricios* Regiment was expanded to four battalions, thus becoming the main foot unit of the Argentine Army. Meanwhile, from April 1830, a new infantry corps had been added to the existing ones. This was initially named "Defenders of Buenos Aires Battalion" but, in June 1835, it received the new denomination of "*Restaurador* Battalion". The two regiments of cavalry created in 1829 were quite short-lived, since they were disbanded in 1832. From the latter year, the Argentine cavalry consisted entirely of militia units except for a few temporary corps that were created over time. The Militia Cavalry of Buenos Aires Province, created as early as 1816, consisted of six regiments by 1830. The latter had four squadrons each (three equipped with lances and one with carbines) and were made up of gauchos. The 1st Regiment was an exception to this rule, since it had six squadrons and comprised also two "extra" squadrons of regular cavalry (made up of soldiers coming from the two disbanded regular cavalry regiments). The 5th Regiment had five squadrons instead of four. The 6th Regiment, commanded by a brother of Rosas, was an elite corps equipped with cuirasses and acting as the mounted guard of the dictator. Each squadron of the six regiments consisted of two companies with 100 men each. In addition to the Militia Regiments, during 1831–1834 the Argentine cavalry also had an elite squadron known as "Governor's Escort". This was disbanded on 4 October 1834, when its members were absorbed into the Carabineer Squadron of the 1st Militia Cavalry Regiment. There was also an independent cavalry corps, known as "Auxiliary Regiment of the Andes", which consisted of two squadrons with two companies each. On 22 March 1831 Rosas created a militarized company of mounted police by assembling together the best policemen who were loyal to his regime. This unit, the "Cavalry Company of Auxiliary Police", became part of the cavalry and acted as a corps of military police. The single artillery battalion consisted of six companies/batteries, the first two of which were mounted. There were also, however, two independent mounted artillery companies that were not attached to the battalion. The latter, in 1835, was reduced in

Argentine grenadier corporal (left) and standard-bearer (right) of the "*Guardia Argentina*" Battalion. *Colour plate by Louis de Beaufort, part of the ASKB Military Collection.*

its numbers and was transformed into a single foot company. As is clear from the above, the Argentine military forces of 1829–1835 continued to consist almost entirely of troops recruited from Buenos Aires Province, since the interior provinces of the state, like Corrientes, were always opposed to the political domination of the capital and thus never provided contingents for the formation of the central army. During the early years of his rule, Rosas created a single company of naval artillery; the *caudillo* later expanded the latter and transformed it into a "brigade" with two companies. He, in addition, also formed a brigade of naval infantry, consisting of two companies, on 4 July 1834.

The military forces of Rosas, 1836–1852

When Argentina commenced hostilities with the Peru-Bolivian Confederation, Rosas had no troops on the north-western borders of his country except for a few local militia units. As a result, he had to form an "Army of Operations" made up of new regular corps recruited in the Andean provinces of Argentina. The new units were the following: 1 battalion of line infantry, 3 companies of light infantry, 1 company of lancers (acting as the mounted bodyguard of the army's commander) and 5 squadrons of cavalry. All these corps were recruited from Jujuy Province and were supported by several militia units coming from the nearby Tucumán Province. By 1840 the Argentine infantry still consisted of two large units, the Argentine Guard Battalion and the *Patricios* Regiment. The first comprised one company of grenadiers, one company of *cazadores*, four companies of fusiliers, one company of artillery and a small detachment of sappers ("*gastadores*"). The second comprised four battalions with six infantry companies and one artillery company each. The *Patricios* Regiment, around 1840, started to be considered as a regular corps. Due to its excellent quality, it was chosen by Rosas to fight against the Anglo-French fleet at the Battle of Vuelta de Obligado. In addition to the two major units described above, during the period 1836–1852 the

Argentine fusiliers of the *"Guardia Argentina"* Battalion, in parade dress (left) and campaign dress (right). *Colour plate by Louis de Beaufort, part of the ASKB Military Collection.*

Argentine infantry comprised some other corps, such as the *"Defensores de la Independencia"* Battalion, created in 1839 by Rosas to support his Uruguayan ally Oribe and being part of the latter's army for several years. The *"Defensores de la Libertad"* Battalion (comprising a small artillery company), was created in 1839 and was part of Oribe's army for a long time. The *"Voluntarios Rebajados"* Battalion, created in 1840, was made up of soldiers whose original units were no longer in existence, the *"Libres Voluntarios de Buenos Aires"* Battalion, was created in 1841 and comprising four companies and the *"Cuartel General"* Battalion, acted as the foot bodyguard of Rosas. There also was a veteran battalion made up of retired soldiers, having garrison duties. The Argentine cavalry continued to consist of the six Militia Regiments, which retained their previous organization (except for the 1st, which reduced its number of regular squadrons from two to one and equipped the latter with cuirasses). In addition, from 1837, Rosas created his own mounted bodyguard known as *"Escolta Libertad"* Regiment. This, despite its denomination, consisted of just two elite companies. The regular cavalry, from 1832, also comprised two units of *"Blandengues"* who were tasked with guarding the frontier of Buenos Aires Province from native incursions. The first unit consisted of two squadrons, while the second had a larger establishment with four squadrons. Finally, in 1840, a single cuirassier unit known as *"Defensores de la Libertad"* Squadron was also added to the regular mounted corps. The artillery, which had been reduced to a single company, was reorganized in 1840 and became a "brigade".

Argentine sapper of the *"Guardia Argentina"* Battalion. *Colour plate by Louis de Beaufort, part of the ASKB Military Collection.*

Argentine grenadier of the *"Patricios"* Regiment. *Colour plate by Louis de Beaufort, part of the ASKB Military Collection.*

The internal enemies of Rosas, 1829–1852

The "*Unitarios*" leader Paz always tried to give some sort of regular organization to the military contingents that were under his command. In 1829 his troops comprised the "*Cazadores de la Libertad*" Battalion, the "*Guardia Republicana*" Battalion, the "*Lanceros Republicanos*" (with three squadrons) and the "*Lanceros Argentinos*" (with three squadrons). These units were later supplemented by the "*Cazadores del Pilar*" Battalion (with five companies), the "*Coraceros de la Guardia de San Juan*" Squadron, the "*Granaderos de la Guardia*" Squadron (made up of Grancolombian deserters coming from Bolivia), the "*Lanceros del Sur*" Squadron and the "*Lanceros de Salta*" (with three squadrons). Lavalle, in 1839, organized his "*Unitarios*" military forces as a single large corps known as "Liberating Legion". This was equipped with the help of the Uruguayan "*Colorados*" and was transported onto Argentine soil by some of the French warships that were blockading the River Plate. Initially it was structured as one mounted bodyguard squadron, five cavalry squadrons, five infantry companies, one company of artillery with two guns and a small reserve. Later the corps was expanded to become a true army by incorporating many militiamen from Corrientes and was reorganized in five legions with two cavalry squadrons each, one infantry battalion ("*Cazadores Correntinos*"), one artillery company with four pieces and two reserve cavalry squadrons. The "*Ejército Grande*" of Urquiza that defeated the military forces of Rosas at the Battle of Caseros, in addition to the Brazilian and Uruguayan troops, comprised the following Argentine units:

Army Corps of Entre Ríos
- Infantry Battalion "*Urquiza*"
- Infantry Battalion "*Entrerriano*"
- 2 Squadrons of Mounted Bodyguard
- 10 Cavalry Divisions
- 1 Squadron of Foot Artillery
- 1 Squadron of Horse Artillery

Argentine drummer of the "*Guardia Argentina*" Battalion (left) and drummer of the "*Patricios*" Regiment (right). *Colour plate by Louis de Beaufort, part of the ASKB Military Collection.*

Army Corps of Corrientes
- Infantry Battalion "*Defensor*"
- Infantry Battalion "*Patricios*"
- 7 Cavalry Divisions
- 1 Squadron of Foot Artillery

Army Corps of Buenos Aires
- Infantry Battalion "Buenos Aires" (former "*Voluntarios Rebajados*" in Rosas' service)
- Infantry Battalion "San Martín" (former 3rd Battalion of the "*Patricios*" in Rosas's service)
- Infantry Battalion "*Constitución*" (former "*Defensores de la Libertad*" in Oribe's service)
- Infantry Battalion "*Federación*" (former "*Defensores de la Independencia*" in Oribe's service)
- 5 Cavalry Divisions
- 2 Squadrons of Foot Artillery

Except for the corps that had previously served under Rosas and Oribe, all the military units listed above were made up of militiamen. The various cavalry "divisions", despite their denomination, were just regiments comprising a variable number of squadrons. After becoming absolute ruler of Argentina, Urquiza demobilized his large army and reorganized the military forces of his country into the following corps: the four infantry battalions of the former "Army Corps of Buenos Aires" and four brand new cavalry regiments (named "*Blandengues*", "Mounted Grenadiers", "Dragoons of the Motherland" and "Hussars of the River Plate").

The Army of the State of Buenos Aires

The new army of the State of Buenos Aires was organized on 18 November 1852. Its infantry consisted of three battalions with six companies each. Of the latter, one was a "*cazadores*" light company whose members were equipped with percussion muskets and not with flintlock ones. In the 3rd Infantry Battalion the "*cazadores*" company was made up of German emigrants living in Buenos Aires. A 4th Infantry Battalion briefly existed during November 1854-February 1855. After being disbanded, it was re-raised on 11 May 1859. The cavalry consisted of three regiments, which had been formed by Urquiza and were retained in service by the new government: 1st Cavalry Regiment "*Blandengues*", 2nd Cavalry Regiment "Mounted Grenadiers" and 3rd Cavalry Regiment "Hussars of the River Plate". Each of them consisted of two squadrons with two companies each. In January 1853 a new cuirassier regiment, named "*Escolta del Gobierno*" and acting as the mounted es-

Argentine private (left) and officer (right) of the "*Defensores de la Independencia*" Battalion. *Colour plate by Louis de Beaufort, part of the ASKB Military Collection.*

cort of the government, was formed. This was later reduced to a single squadron before being disbanded in 1855. During the latter year the line cavalry was expanded with the formation of the new 4th Cavalry Regiment "Dragoons of Buenos Aires", which was soon followed by the 5th Cavalry Regiment and 6th Cavalry Regiment. In 1857 the "*Escolta del Gobierno*" Squadron was re-raised and was later expanded to become a regiment in 1859. The artillery of the State of Buenos Aires consisted of the "Light Artillery Regiment", which was formed by two squadrons of mounted artillery with two companies/batteries each. In 1853 the corps was reorganized as the "Artillery Division of Buenos Aires", consisting of two autonomous "brigades", one of positional artillery and one of mounted artillery. In 1859 the brigade of mounted artillery became again an autonomous unit as the "Light Artillery Regiment" (with two squadrons having two companies each). In 1860 an independent squadron of light artillery was formed for service on the southern frontier of Buenos Aires against the natives. Since 1853 the State of Buenos Aires also had a single company of naval infantry, which was transformed into a "Brigade of Naval Infantry" with two companies in 1859. The corps, almost entirely composed of European emigrants, was disbanded in 1861.

In September 1852 the government of the State of Buenos Aires disbanded all the existing militia units and replaced them with a new National Guard. This would comprise a small number of regular soldiers inside each of its units, in order to provide the militiamen with some solid military instruction. By 1857 the National Guard consisted of 4 infantry regiments recruited from the inhabitants of Buenos Aires, having two battalions each. These were well trained and could be supplemented, in case of need, by several National Guard units recruited from the countryside of the State of Buenos Aires. The military forces of the latter also comprised several units of volunteers, mostly made up of foreign emigrants. In 1852, when Urquiza besieged Buenos Aires, the Italians living in the city, several of whom had been part of Garibaldi's Italian Legion that fought during the Siege of Montevideo, organized a new "Italian Legion" consisting of two infantry companies. The latter distinguished itself in combat and was awarded the new denomination of "*Valiente Legión Italiana*" ("Valorous Italian Legion"). The corps was gradually expanded to comprise three companies of fusiliers, one company of "*bersaglieri*" (light infantry), one company of cavalry, one company of artillery and one reserve company. It was disbanded on 14 August 1853. In 1855 the government of Buenos Aires decided to create a settlement inhabited by Italian military colonists at Bahía Blanca, on the "indian frontier" of its territory. The Italian emigrants who moved into the borders of Buenos Aires' countryside were thus organized as a military unit known as "*Legión Agricola Militar*", which consisted of two companies of infantrymen, one company of "*bersaglieri*", one company of cavalry, one company of artillery and one detachment of engineers. In 1864, after having fought with courage during the campaigns of 1859 and 1861, the Italian Legion of Bahía Blanca was transformed into a standard regular infantry battalion of the Argentine Army and received the new denomination of "*Legión Militar*". Meanwhile in April 1861, with new emigrants coming from Italy, the State of Buenos Aires had formed a new "foreign corps" named "*Legión Voluntarios de la Libertad*". This, consisting of four infantry companies, soon started to include emigrants coming from various European nations and thus was briefly re-named "*Legión Extranjera*" ("Foreign Legion") in May 1862. The military forces of the State of Buenos Aires also comprised a "German Legion" consisting of one infantry company and one artillery detachment, created in January 1853 and soon attached to the 3rd Infantry Battalion, a "Spanish Legion", consisting of a single infantry company and serving during the Siege of Buenos Aires and a "Legion of Volunteer Swiss Riflemen", consisting of two companies of Swiss emigrants who served during the Siege of Buenos Aires.

The Army of the Argentine Confederation

The Argentine Confederation of Urquiza had quite a large army, which was organized in a more "traditional" way if compared with that of the State of Buenos Aires. Its infantry consisted of just three battalions (reduced to two in 1856) with four companies each and of nine weak independent companies that performed garrison duties. The cavalry, instead, was much stronger and comprised the following corps: one "*Escolta*" Squadron acting as the mounted bodyguard of Urquiza,

Argentine officer (left) and private (right) of the "*Defensores de la Libertad*" Battalion. *Colour plate by Louis de Beaufort, part of the ASKB Military Collection.*

eight regiments of dragoons (equipped as lancers) with two or three squadrons each, one "Mounted Grenadiers" Regiment acting as frontier cavalry and eleven independent companies performing garrison duties. In 1856, after the mounted units listed above completed their formation, they were reorganized as nine cavalry regiments numbered 1-9 and in 1860 a 10th Cavalry Regiment was added to the existing ones. The artillery of the Argentine Confederation initially consisted of one field brigade with two companies, one independent field company, one horse company and one positional company. In 1859 another two companies of field artillery were created. The capital of the Argentine Confederation, Paraná, had a National Guard, formed on 5 May 1856, that consisted of one infantry regiment with two battalions.

The Argentine Army of Mitre

The new Argentine Army that emerged after the Battle of Pavón was formed on the basis of the victorious military forces of the State of Buenos Aires. On 26 January 1864 Mitre signed a Presidential Decree that completely reorganized the latter. According to this, the regular forces were to be organized into the following corps: six infantry battalions, eight cavalry regiments and one artillery regiment. Each unit, regardless of branch, was to have an establishment of 400 soldiers. According to the new organization, each infantry battalion had 5 companies of 80 men, one of grenadiers, one of "*cazadores*" and three of fusiliers. Each cavalry regiment had four squadrons with 100 men, divided into two companies. The Regiment of Artillery was organized in two squadrons with two batteries each and only had light horse-drawn guns. Garrisoning the "Indian Frontier" there were 11 independent companies of infantry, 5 independent companies of artillery and some independent squadrons/

Argentine standard-bearer of the "*Restaurador*" Battalion. *Colour plate by Louis de Beaufort, part of the ASKB Military Collection.*

companies of cavalry. Each of the latter frontier units could comprise no more than 600 soldiers.

With the outbreak of the Paraguayan War, Mitre was forced to decree a "Siege Status and War Situation" order, in response to the Paraguayan declaration of war on 16 April 1865. As a result, the so-called "Army of the Line" was increased to 10,000 soldiers, organized into 11 infantry battalions, 8 cavalry regiments and 1 regiment of artillery. All the infantry battalions (numbered 1, 2, 3, 4, 5, 6, 7, 8, 9, 11 and 12) were increased in size to six companies with 80 men each. The "*Legión Militar*" became the new 8th Infantry Battalion. On 20 April 1865 a Company of "*Zapadores*" (Sappers) was added to the Argentine regular forces, being composed of 100 volunteers from the National Guard of Buenos Aires, who were commanded by Colonel Cetz, a Polish officer in the service of Argentina. On 1 June 1865 the unit was expanded and became the "Battalion of Engineers". It is interesting to note that Cetz not only commanded the original company, but also picked its officers and acquired all the needed equipment, including artillery observer balloons bought from the United States (the first military baloons ever used in South America). On 26 April 1865 the mounted "Escort to the Governor" was formed, in order to protect Mitre during the military operations. It had two squadrons of 100 men, taken respectively from the 1st and 3rd Cavalry Regiments. With the declaration of war, Mitre was obliged to remobilize the National Guard forces in order to draft them into the regular army and increase its size. On 17 April 1865, he declared the formation of the "National Army on Campaign", which included the 10,000 soldiers of the regular army plus 15,000 men from the National Guard. In total, this new force was to comprise 30 infantry battalions (11 of the line and 19 of the National Guard) with 500 soldiers in each battalion. Mitre also determined the quantity of the contingents that each province should form and that were sent to the capital for the war effort. Service in the National Guard was made compulsory for all married men between the ages of 17–45 and bachelors aged 17–50 by a law of 5 June 1865.

Argentine officer of the regular cavalry squadrons attached to the 1st Militia Cavalry Regiment. *Colour plate by Louis de Beaufort, part of the ASKB Military Collection.*

Argentine trooper of the regular cavalry squadrons attached to the 1st Militia Cavalry Regiment. *Colour plate by Louis de Beaufort, part of the ASKB Military Collection.*

Uniforms and weapons

The uniforms worn by the Argentine Army during the Cisplatine War came into use following the promulgation of new dress regulations on 18 August 1826. The latter tried to "make order" of the uniforms of the Argentine Army, after anarchy had reigned for several years during the last phase of the Wars of Independence. For the M1826 dress of the Argentine Army see the relevant pictures and captions. Its general appearance was still very "Napoleonic". The 3rd Infantry Battalion, which later became the nucleus of the Uruguayan Army, was the only one wearing yellow "*sardinetas*" (pointed stripes of cloth) on the collar and cuffs. The musket used by all infantrymen was the Brown Bess, the standard weapon of the Argentine foot troops during the period 1825–1852. The Presidential Escort made up of former members of the glorious "*Granaderos a Caballo*" was uniformed like the line cavalry regiments, but with a yellow flaming grenade badge on the collar. The 4th Line Cavalry Regiment, "Lavalle's Cuirassiers", was dressed in dark blue with metal cuirasses. Its troopers used a standard line cavalry shako instead of the peaked cap worn by officers. The "Hussars Defenders of the National Honour" were uniformed like the standard line cavalry units, while the "Cuirassiers of the Guard" looked practically identical to "Lavalle's Cuirassiers". The 16th Line Cavalry Regiment, "Olavarría's Lancers", wore a distinctive hussar-style dress in green that was quite similar to that of the "*Cazadores a Caballo de los Andes*" (a glorious Argentine military corps that had participated in the Wars of Independence). The M1826 uniforms of the Argentine artillery consisted of black shako with brass front plate and national cockade, dark blue single-breasted coat with red piping to collar and round cuffs, yellow flaming grenade badge embroidered

Argentine trooper of the "*Escolta Libertad*" Regiment. *Colour plate by Louis de Beaufort, part of the ASKB Military Collection.*

on the collar, dark blue trousers with red side-stripe and white belt equipment. The newly-formed Regiment of Light Artillery was dressed in a similar way, but being a horse artillery corps it used black leather grenadier boots.

During the long years of Rosas' rule most units of the Argentine Army were dressed with a "regularized" version of the traditional gaucho costume, which comprised the following four basic elements: *gorrete* (a soft cap with a long strip of cloth wrapped around its main body and ending with a tassel), single-breasted loose jacket or blouse, *chiripá* (a poncho worn wrapped around the hips) and white *calzoncillos* (embroidered trousers, used as a sort of undergarment). The "*Cazadores* of the River Plate" Battalion, the "*Guardia Argentina*" Battalion and the "*Patricios*" Regiment were the only units of the Argentine infantry to have uniforms of standard European cut, showing a distinctive French influence. The short-lived "*Cazadores* of the River Plate" were uniformed as follows: dark blue shako with red plume, brass front plate, national cockade, red cords and flounders, dark blue coat with red collar having white piping, dark blue round cuffs with red piping, red frontal lapels piped in white, red turnbacks with yellow bugle horn badge, dark blue trousers with red side-stripe and white belt equipment. The first uniform of the "*Guardia Argentina*" Battalion consisted of the following elements: dark blue shako with white plume having red point, brass front plate, national cockade, white cords and flounders, dark blue coat with red collar having one yellow "*sardineta*" and green piping, dark blue round cuffs with green piping and three yellow "*sardinetas*", white lapels piped in green, red turnbacks with yellow bugle horn badge, dark blue trousers with green side-stripe and white belt equipment. In 1840 the new dress shown in one of the pictures came into use. This included a black bearskin, with red plume and bag as well as a brass flaming grenade on the front, and red loose trousers for the grenadiers of the unit. During 1835–1843 the "*Patricios*" were dressed with a "gaucho" uniform consisting of dark blue *gorrete* with red piping and white tassel, dark blue jacket with red collar and cuffs, dark blue trousers with red side-stripe. In 1843 they adopted the new "European" uniform shown in one of the pictures, with red trousers. In 1847 a new and more traditional uniform came into use: red *gorrete* with white piping and tassel bearing white battalion number on the front, red jacket with dark blue collar and cuffs piped in white, two white "*sardinetas*" on collar, red *bombachas* (loose trousers) and white belt equipment. The "*Restaurador*" Battalion wore black round hats with red plume and national cockade, red jacket with white piping to collar and round cuffs, dark blue trousers and white belt equipment. For the "*Defensores de la Independencia*" and "*Defensores de la Libertad*" see the relevant pictures and captions. The "*Voluntarios Rebajados*" had red *gorrete*, dark blue jacket with red facings and dark blue trousers with red side-stripe. The "*Libres Voluntarios de Buenos Aires*" and the "*Cuartel General*" Battalion wore uniforms that were almost identical to that adopted by the "*Patricios*" in 1847.

For the uniforms of Rosas' regular and militia cavalry units, see the relevant pictures. The 1st Militia Cavalry Regiment employed a peculiar uniform: black shako with red pompom and white cord, red jacket with three rows of white metal buttons on the front, dark blue collar and pointed cuffs piped in white, two white bars on the collar, dark blue trousers with red side-stripe. The two short-lived regular regiments of 1829–1832 were equipped with metal cuirasses and wore red *gorretes* together with dark blue jackets. The Governor's Escort disbanded in 1834 was dressed similarly, but with black shako and red jacket. The "Auxiliary Regiment of the Andes" had a black busby with red side-bag, dark blue jacket with red facings (green for the single light company of "*flanqueadores*") and dark blue trousers with red or green side-stripe. The "*Blandengues*" created in 1832 wore red *gorrete*, dark blue jacket with red collar and cuffs, red *chiripá* and white *calzoncillos*. The "*Defensores de la Libertad*" Squadron was uniformed in the same way, but with dark blue *chiripá*. Rosas' artillery

Argentine trooper of the 6th Militia Cavalry Regiment. *Colour plate by Louis de Beaufort, part of the ASKB Military Collection.*

was dressed as follows: dark blue shako with brass front plate, red cords-and-flounders, red plume, dark blue jacket with red facings and yellow flaming grenade on collar, dark blue trousers with red side-stripe and white belt equipment. In 1844 the colours of the jacket and of the trousers were inverted. The naval infantry was uniformed as follows: dark blue visored cap with brass front badge (an anchor), dark blue single-breasted coat with red collar and pointed cuffs, single white *sardineta* on the collar, red *bombachas* and white belt equipment. The naval artillery had: black shako with brass anchor badge, red plume, red cords-and-flounders; red single-breasted coat with dark blue collar and round cuffs piped in white, red *bombachas* and white belt equipment. A distinctive red ribbon was worn by all the "*Federales*" troops during Rosas' period of rule, usually on the chest.

The "*Unitarios*" of General Paz were, in most cases, well uniformed. The "*Cazadores de la Libertad*" and the "*Guardia Republicana*" had black shako and dark blue coatee with green facings, the first unit with yellow piping, the second with white piping. The "*Cazadores de la Libertad*" had yellow *sardinetas* on the cuffs. The "*Lanceros Republicanos*" and "*Lanceros Argentinos*" had dark blue visorless cap with green bottom band and dark blue jacket with green facings. The "*Lanceros del Sur*" had dark blue visorless cap with light blue bottom band and dark blue jacket with light blue facings. For the uniform of the infantry of Lavalle's Legion see the relevant picture and caption. The cavalry, instead, was dressed as follows: dark blue visored Carlist cap with light blue bottom band, dark blue blouse with light blue folded collar and cuffs, light blue pocket flaps and strip placed under the front buttons, dark blue trousers and light blue pennon of the lance. The artillery was dressed in the same way, but with the blouse having reversed colours. The Argentine units of Urquiza's "*Ejército Grande*" did not wear proper military uniforms and were dressed in the usual "gaucho" style, all their garments were red. For more details about their dress, see the relevant pictures and captions. The excellent cavalry of Entre Ríos, like the rest of Urquiza's mounted troops, was uniformed with red *gorrete* or round visorless cap that was worn together with a blouse or a jacket of the same colour. Since Rosas' Regiments of Militia Cavalry were dressed very similarly, all the horsemen of Urquiza wore a white *chaleco* or waistcoat over their jacket/blouse. The infantry and the artillery did not use this special garment.

Argentine trooper of the 6th Militia Cavalry Regiment.
Colour plate by Louis de Beaufort, part of the ASKB Military Collection.

The Army of the State of Buenos Aires wore uniforms that were close copies of the contemporary French ones, while the Army of the Argentine Confederation was mostly dressed with "traditional" uniforms that were quite similar to those used under Rosas. The military forces of the Argentine Confederation were mostly dressed with dark blue *gorrete* (having red piping and tassel) and dark blue blouse or jacket having red facings. The jacket/blouse could have red pocket flaps, stripe under the front buttons and piece of cloth on the shoulders. Officers had a dark blue képi or visored cap as headgear, with golden piping showing rank. For more details on this "general issue" uniform, see the relevant picture. The "*Escolta*" Squadron (also known as "*Estrella*" Squadron) and the "Mounted Grenadiers" Regiment were the only ones to use uniforms of European cut. The first wore red shako with brass front plate and fittings, white falling plume and cords-and-flounders, red tunic with dark blue frontal plastron and golden epaulettes, metal cuirass painted in black and worn over a red *fraise*, dark blue trousers with red side-stripe and white belt equipment. The second wore dark blue képi with national cockade, red falling plume, red bottom band and piping, dark blue tunic with red frontal plastron, dark blue collar with yellow flaming grenade badge, red pointed cuffs, golden contre-epaulettes, dark blue trousers with red side-stripe and black belt equipment.

The military forces of the State of Buenos Aires were dressed according to the regulations promulgated on 19 September 1853, which were clearly influenced by the French regulations of 1852. For the uniforms of infantry and cavalry see the relevant pictures. In 1855 the 1st Infantry Battalion, being considered the heir of the glorious "*Patricios*", was given permission to have a red shako instead of the usual black one. The uniform of the artillery corps, which changed denomination several times, consisted of emerald green képi and single-breasted jacket with red facings. The independent squadron of light (mounted) artillery created in 1860 was dressed as follows: dark blue képi with red bottom band and piping, dark blue single-breasted tunic with red collar and pointed cuffs, dark blue trousers with red side-stripe and black belt equipment. The "*Escolta del Gobierno*" Squadron originally wore white metal helmet and cuirass (imported from France, the former with black tuft and horsehair mane), red *fraise*, dark blue single-breasted tunic with red collar and pointed cuffs, red trousers with dark blue

---

Argentine trooper of the Militia Cavalry Regiments. *Colour plate by Louis de Beaufort, part of the ASKB Military Collection.*

Argentine trooper of the 2nd Militia Cavalry Regiment. *Colour plate by Louis de Beaufort, part of the ASKB Military Collection.*

Argentine trooper of the 2nd Militia Cavalry Regiment. *Colour plate by Louis de Beaufort, part of the ASKB Military Collection.*

side-stripe and white belt equipment. In 1859, after becoming a regiment, the corps was given the dark blue uniform with yellow facings that was later adopted by the 3rd Cavalry Regiment of the Argentine Army (see relevant picture). The Brigade of Naval Infantry was dressed like the line infantry but with red facings. For the uniforms of the National Guard infantry, see the relevant picture and caption. These, consisting of képi and blouse, were worn also by the line infantry on campaign, but with green facings instead of the red ones. The National Guard cavalry wore red "bag" soft caps with dark blue bottom band and dark blue blouses with red facings (identical to those of the infantry). The outfit was completed by *chiripá* and *calzoncillos*. The line cavalry on campaign was uniformed in the same way, but with dark blue képi having red bottom band and piping as headgear. The "*Valiente Legión Italiana*" was dressed with black "*Bersaglieri*" wide-brimmed hat having capercaillie feathers, dark blue double-breasted tunic with green collar and pointed cuffs, green piping to front, dark blue trousers with green side-stripe and black belt equipment. The later "*Legión Agricola Militar*" wore a simpler uniform that was almost identical to that of Buenos Aires' National Guard infantry. The infantry companies had dark blue képi with red bottom band and piping, while those of cavalry and artillery had red képi with dark blue bottom band and piping. The single company of "*Bersaglieri*" wore the typical hat that had been previously used by the "*Valiente Legión Italiana*". The "*Legión Voluntarios de la Libertad*" wore red képi with green bottom band and piping together with the same blouse and trousers of the "*Legión Agricola Militar*" but with green facings instead of red ones. The "Spanish Legion" had white Carlist cap with black tassel, dark blue double-breasted tunic with green collar (having yellow bugle horn badge) and pointed cuffs, dark blue trousers with green side-stripe and black belt equipment. The Volunteer Swiss riflemen were uniformed like the Nation-

---

Argentine officer of the Cavalry Company of Auxiliary Police. *Colour plate by Louis de Beaufort, part of the ASKB Military Collection.*

al Guard infantry, but in grey with green facings. The unified Argentine Army re-formed after 1861 was given uniforms that were almost identical to those used by the military forces of the State of Buenos Aires. No new dress regulations were promulgated and thus the slight modifications introduced after 1861 were "formalized" only with the promulgation of the first dress regulations of the unified Argentine Army in 1871. French style was at that time dominant among South American armies, most of which copied the uniforms of Napoleon III's military forces. In Argentina's case, many of the army's provisions were surplus from the Imperial Army coming directly from France. During the Paraguayan War, great quantities of cloth, kepis and equipment were bought from French manufacturers.

Before the Paraguayan War, the Argentine Army employed a bewildering variety of muzzle-loading flintlock and percussion muskets. This situation was a real nightmare for the supply branch and caused many problems during the conflict of 1864–1870. The most common infantry weapon was the Brown Bess musket, locally known as "Tower" because it bore the inspection seal of the Tower of London arsenal. More than 11,000 of these flintlock muskets had been captured from the British during the invasions of 1806–1807. With the exception of the battalions from Buenos Aires (which had percussion muskets, like the majority of the regulars), all the National Guard infantrymen were armed with the Brown Bess. The percussion muskets, smoothbores or rifles, were of different makes and calibers, including 18mm French M1842T, French Minié M1851, 18mm Norwegian M1842, 17.8 mm Thouvenin M1853 ("*carabine à tige*") and 18mm Alem M1842 (manufactured in Germany, issued to the National Guard infantry of Buenos Aires). A certain number of the bayonets (1,000) were French Saint-Etienne ones. In December 1865, six Pattern 1853 Enfields were dispatched to the front for evaluation. As a result of their good performance, a certain number of them was bought. Regarding pistols, percussion models were very common by 1865, mostly 17.8 mm French M1822T or Prussian M1840, but Austrian and Belgian handguns were also in use. Revolvers, however, became soon dominant. The most common were the Lefaucheux ones (model 1858, 1859 or 1863), but also Adams and Webley revolvers were used. The cavalry employed many different types of carbines: Tower (Brown Bess), 18mm French M1829T Bis (known as "*Vincennes*"), 18mm French M1842T, 18mm Belgian M1842T and 18mm French M1840 muskets cut down as carbines. In addition, a certain number of Pattern 1856 Enfield cavalry carbines and Pattern 1861 Enfield musketoons were also in use by 1865. The regular cavalry had a certain number of Prussian model 1852 sabers, but the majority of the Argentine cavalrymen (especially of the National Guard) were armed with old stirrup-hilted (Pattern 1796 for light cavalry) British sabers. Lances were the main weapon of the Argentine cavalry, with conventional models being used by the regulars and gaucho spears being very common among National Guardsmen (especially among the irregular cavalry from Corrientes). Obviously the "bolas" were also very popular.

Argentine trooper of the Cavalry Company of Auxiliary Police. *Colour plate by Louis de Beaufort, part of the ASKB Military Collection.*

Argentine infantryman of General Paz's military forces. *Colour plate by Louis de Beaufort, part of the ASKB Military Collection.*

Argentine infantry officer (left) and private (right) of General Lavalle's military forces. *Colour plate by Louis de Beaufort, part of the ASKB Military Collection.*

Infantryman of General Urquiza's army. *Colour plate by Louis de Beaufort, part of the ASKB Military Collection.*

Cavalryman of General Urquiza's army. *Colour plate by Louis de Beaufort, part of the ASKB Military Collection.*

Cavalryman of General Urquiza's army. *Colour plate by Francisco Ferrer Llul, part of the ASKB Military Collection.*

Uniforms of the Argentine Confederation's regular cavalry. *Colour plate by Louis de Beaufort, part of the ASKB Military Collection.*

Line infantryman of the State of Buenos Aires in parade dress. *Colour plate by Louis de Beaufort, part of the ASKB Military Collection.*

Private (left) and officer (right) of the State of Buenos Aires' line infantry in campaign dress. *Colour plate by Louis de Beaufort, part of the ASKB Military Collection.*

Trooper of the State of Buenos Aires' cavalry in parade dress. *Colour plate by Louis de Beaufort, part of the ASKB Military Collection.*

Uniforms of the State of Buenos Aires' National Guard infantry. *Colour plate by Louis de Beaufort, part of the ASKB Military Collection.*

The Uruguayan Army

History and organization

Soon after launching their rebellion against the Empire of Brazil in the summer of 1825, Lavalleja and the other Uruguayan patriot leaders tried to organize their insurgent forces in a proper way. As a result, the following units were formed: "*Libertos Orientales*" Battalion, "*Dragones Orientales*" Regiment, "*Dragones de la Unión*" Regiment, "*Dragones Libertadores*" Regiment, "*Húsares Orientales*" Regiment, "*Tiradores de la Patria*" Squadron and "*del Orden*" Squadron. These regular corps were supported by a sizeable number of irregular militiamen, as well as by some artillery pieces. The "*Libertos Orientales*" Battalion was the only infantry corps of the army and had been recruited from free blacks living in the department of Florida. This unit was of excellent quality and thus was later absorbed into the Argentine Army as the 3rd Infantry Battalion. Also the "*Dragones Orientales*" Regiment, commanded by Oribe, was a well-disciplined corps and thus it was absorbed into the Argentine Army as the 9th Cavalry Regiment. The "*Tiradores de la Patria*" Squadron was the only unit of the Uruguayan cavalry whose members were all equipped with flintlock carbines. After Uruguay became an independent republic, on 24 February 1829, the Uruguayan Army was officially created. It was to comprise the following corps: 1 light infantry battalion, 3 cavalry regiments, 1 mounted bodyguard squadron and 1 brigade of artillery. On 27 February 1830 this structure was slightly altered, since the cavalry was reduced to three squadrons and the artillery to a single company. The light infantry battalion was nothing other than the former 3rd Infantry Battalion of the Argentine Army, which started to be known as "Florida" Battalion. It comprised six companies.

Uruguayan trooper of the "*Dragones Orientales*". *Colour plate by Louis de Beaufort, part of the ASKB Military Collection.*

Uruguayan trooper of the *"Dragones de la Unión"*. *Colour plate by Louis de Beaufort, part of the ASKB Military Collection.*

The "*Blancos*" military forces of Oribe, 1836–1851

When the "*Guerra Grande*" broke out between "*Blancos*" and "*Colorados*" in 1836 the few existing regular units, described above, remained loyal to the government of Oribe but were soon completely destroyed during the early engagements of the conflict. As a result, the leader of the Uruguayan conservatives had to re-build his military forces almost from zero, with the decisive support of his ally Rosas. By March 1843 the joint Argentine-Uruguayan army besieging Rivera in Montevideo consisted of the following corps:
- 1st Infantry Regiment (Uruguayan)
- 4th Infantry Regiment (Uruguayan)
- "*Escolta*" Battalion (Uruguayan)
- "*Defensores de la Independencia Oriental*" Battalion (Uruguayan)
- "*Cazadores Orientales*" Battalion (Uruguayan)
- "*Libertad*" Battalion (Argentine)
- "*Independencia*" Battalion (Argentine)
- 3rd Battalion of the "*Patricios*" Regiment (Argentine)
- "*Libres Voluntarios de Buenos Aires*" Battalion (Argentine)
- "*Voluntarios Rebajados*" Battalion (Argentine)
- "*Escolta Restauradora*" Squadron (Uruguayan)
- "*Lanceros de Linea*" Squadron (Uruguayan)
- "*Dragones de Buenos Aires*" Squadron (Argentine)
- Artillery Brigade, with two companies (Uruguayan)

As is clear from the above, Rosas' men formed the backbone of Oribe's regular forces. The latter were supplemented by four "divisions" of militiamen, each comprising from 400 to 800 men.

The "*Colorados*" military forces of Rivera, 1836–1851

Rivera, trapped inside Montevideo for eight years, recruited his military forces from the inhabitants of the Uruguayan capital. The latter, in 1843, had a population of 31,189 individuals that comprised several foreign communities, including 5,324 French, 4,205 Italians, 3,406 Spaniards, 2,553 Argentines (mostly "*Unitarios*" refugees) and 1,344 blacks. All these "minorities" contributed to the defence of Montevideo by forming their own military units. In 1839 the "*Colorados*" military corps comprised the following: four infantry battalions ("*Infantería de Línea*", "*Voluntarios*", "*Orden*" and

Uruguayan troopers of the "*Húsares Orientales*" (left) and of the "*Tiradores de la Patria*" (right). *Colour plate by Louis de Beaufort, part of the ASKB Military Collection.*

"*Matrícula*"), one battalion of National Guard, one battalion of Urban Militia, one line cavalry squadron, one militia cavalry squadron (acting as mounted bodyguard of Rivera), one company of Argentine volunteers, 800 militarized policemen and 250 men of the so-called "*Guardia Nacional de Extramuros*" (national guardsmen coming from the countryside around Montevideo). By 1843 the military forces of Rivera had been greatly expanded and consisted of the following: five regular infantry battalions (the 4th of which was entirely made up of free blacks), one regiment (with three battalions) and nine battalions of National Guard infantry, one regular cavalry squadron, one regiment (with three squadrons) and six squadrons of National Guard cavalry, one battalion of positional artillery, one squadron of field artillery and several irregular corps. Of the nine National Guard infantry battalions one consisted of militarized policemen, one was made up of Spanish volunteers (the "*Aguerridos*" Battalion) and one was recruited from the countryside of Montevideo (the "*Extramuros*" Battalion). Of the six National Guard cavalry squadrons one consisted of black lancers equipped with cuirasses, one of white cuirassiers and one of white lancers. These all acted as the mounted bodyguard of Rivera.

In addition to the units listed above there were the three autonomous "legions of foreigners": the French Legion, the Italian Legion and the Argentine Legion. A first unit of French volunteers had been formed as early as 1839, while the French warships were blockading the River Plate. This small corps, commanded by the brother of the French consul in Montevideo, was soon disbanded. In February 1843 the French Legion was created with the official title of "*Defensores de la Libertad*" Battalion. This, commanded by Colonel Jean-Chrysostome Thiebaut who was a veteran of the Napoleonic Wars, performed extremely well and was rapidly expanded. It came to comprise three infantry battalions (each with one grenadier company, one light company and four centre companies), one brigade of artillery with two companies and a detachment of "*zapadores*". Later the French Legion also absorbed a "Basque Legion" that had been formed by the Catalan and Basque emigrants living in Montevideo. The latter did not want to serve with the other Spanish volunteers due to the ongoing Carlist Wars and thus formed two autonomous companies that were subsequently expanded to become a new battalion of the French Legion. The latter, despite its great quality, was disbanded on 11 April 1844. The Italian Legion was formed on 20 April 1843, by assembling together two companies of Italians that were already in existence. Command of the new unit was soon assumed by Giuseppe Garibaldi, who had been a hero of the Riograndense Republic and who also commanded the naval forces of the "*Colorados*". The 700 Italian volunteers were organized in three battalions, which included a company of naval infantry and a small artillery detachment. The Italian Legion, unlike the French one, continued to exist until the end of the "Great Siege" and was disbanded only on 12 October 1851 (after having been reduced to a single battalion with eight companies). The Argentine Legion consisted of a single infantry battalion, made up of "*Unitarios*" political refugees who lived in Montevideo. During 1843 the various infantry forces of Rivera's army were assembled together in order to form three brigades, each of which consisted of four battalions. In July 1851 the Uruguayan "*Colorados*" reorganized their troops on the following units: three battalions of regular infantry ("*Resistencia*", "*Voltijeros*" and "*Guardia Oriental*") with six companies each, two battalions of National Guard infantry, one detachment of mounted bodyguard, one battalion of field artillery, one squadron of horse artillery and a corps of supernumerary officers.

Uruguayan private of the "*Florida*" Battalion", wearing the uniform of the Argentine 3rd Infantry Battalion in 1828. *Colour plate by Francisco Ferrer Llul, part of the ASKB Military Collection.*

The Uruguayan Army of 1852–1865

The "*Ejército Grande*" of Urquiza that defeated Rosas at Caseros comprised an "expeditionary division" provided by Uruguay, which consisted of the following units: Battalion "*Resistencia*", Battalion "*Voltijeros*", Battalion "*Guardia Oriental*", Battalion "*Orden*", Mounted Bodyguard Detachment and Horse Artillery Squadron. The Battalion "*Orden*" was the only newly-formed corps, which was created from the remnants of the glorious Italian Legion. After the fall of Rosas, to cut economic costs, three of the existing infantry battalions ("*Resistencia*", "*Guardia Oriental*" and "*Orden*") were disbanded and their members were assembled together to form the new Battalion "*Cazadores de la Unión*". The "*Voltijeros*" were the 1st Infantry Battalion, the "*Cazadores*" were the 2nd Infantry Battalion. In addition to the above there still were the Mounted Bodyguard Detachment, the Artillery Battalion and the Horse Artillery Squadron. In 1858, due to the increasing tension between "*Colorados*" and "*Blancos*", the two battalions of regular infantry were disbanded and were replaced by

Uruguayan sergeant of the regular infantry (left) and militiaman of the militia infantry (right), uniformed according to the 1829 dress regulations. *Colour plate by Louis de Beaufort, part of the ASKB Military Collection.*

the reorganized National Guard. Already in 1859, however, one regular "Urban Company" of infantry had been created to act as the garrison of Montevideo. In 1860 a single regular infantry battalion, known as 1st *Cazadores* Battalion, was raised. When Flores launched his "*Cruzada Libertadora*" the regular Uruguayan military forces remained loyal to the central government and thus he had to organize his own troops from zero, by assembling them in two infantry battalions named "*Florida*" and "*24 de Abril*". Flores could also count on a battalion, named "*Voluntarios Garibaldinos*", which was recruited by the Brazilians in Uruguay after their intervention. This, made up of four companies, mostly consisted of Italian volunteers and with the outbreak of the Paraguayan War it became part of the Brazilian Army. The ruling "*Blancos*" hastily expanded their troops by raising a new "*Defensores*" Battalion consisting of just two companies, but all their forces disappeared following the fall of Paysandú. After the end of the Uruguayan War, Flores reorganized his army in the following units: "*Florida*" Battalion, "*24 de Abril*" Battalion, Mounted Bodyguard Detachment and Horse Artillery Squadron. In May 1865, after signing the "Triple Alliance Treaty" with Brazil and Argentina, the Uruguayan government was required to form a "division" that would have fought against Paraguay. As a result, two new infantry battalions were created and the horse artillery corps was expanded to become a regiment with two squadrons. The two new foot battalions were named "*Voluntarios de la Libertad*" and "*Voluntarios de la Patria*". The first was made up of former national guardsmen from Montevideo, the latter of former national guardsmen from the rest of Uruguay. The Uruguayan Division sent to Paraguay in 1865 comprised the four infantry battalions, the Mounted Bodyguard Detachment and the 2nd Squadron of the Horse Artillery Regiment.

Uruguayan officer (left) and trooper (right) of the regular cavalry, uniformed according to the 1829 dress regulations.
Colour plate by Louis de Beaufort, part of the ASKB Military Collection.

Uniforms and weapons

The Uruguayan military forces of 1825 were dressed in very simple uniforms. For those of the "*Dragones de la Unión*" and "*Dragones Orientales*" see the relevant pictures. The "*Libertos Orientales*" had red "bag" caps, dark blue jackets with red facings, red *chiripá* and white *calzoncillos*. The "*Dragones Libertadores*" wore dark blue visorless cap with yellow bottom band, dark blue jacket with yellow facings and dark blue trousers with yellow side-stripe. The "*Húsares Orientales*" had dark blue visorless cap with red bottom band, red blouse with dark blue facings, dark blue *chiripá* and white *calzoncillos*. The "*Tiradores de la Patria*" had dark blue visorless cap with light blue bottom band, dark blue jacket with light blue facings and dark blue trousers with light blue side-stripe. For the early uniforms of the Uruguayan Army introduced with the dress regulations of 1829, see the relevant pictures and captions. In 1831 the uniform of the infantry was modified. See the relevant picture.

The standard uniform worn by the Uruguayan infantry and artillery units of Oribe's Army consisted of red "*bonnet de police*", jacket/blouse and *chiripá* worn together with white *calzoncillos*. The cavalry was dressed quite similarly, entirely in

Uruguayan trooper of the regular cavalry, uniformed according to the 1829 dress regulations. *Colour plate by Louis de Beaufort, part of the ASKB Military Collection.*

Uruguayan artilleryman (left) and engineer officer (right), uniformed according to the 1829 dress regulations. *Colour plate by Louis de Beaufort, part of the ASKB Military Collection.*

red, but with *gorrete* instead of the bonnet de police. Officers usually wore a dark blue visorless cap with golden bottom band and tassel, red single-breasted coat with short tails and golden epaulettes, dark blue trousers with golden side-stripe. The infantry of Rivera's Army was dressed in an extremely simple way: dark blue *bonnet de police* with red piping and tassel, white single-breasted jacket with standing collar, white trousers and white belt equipment. The 4th Line Infantry Battalion, being made up of free black soldiers, was an exception to this rule since it wore a distinctive uniform with dark green coat having yellow facings. The small regular cavalry of Rivera's Army wore dark blue visorless caps with yellow bottom band and tassel, dark blue jacket with yellow facings and dark blue trousers with yellow side-stripe. The three National Guard cavalry squadrons acting as the mounted bodyguard of the Colorados' leader wore peculiar uniforms. The Cuirassier Squadron was dressed with an elegant French-style uniform, which was produced in a white version for summer (see relevant picture). For the uniforms of the black lancers ("*Camacho*" Squadron) and of the white lancers ("*Voluntarios de la Independencia*" Squadron) see the relevant pictures. The artillery was dressed with light blue visorless cap having red tassel and bottom band, red blouse with light blue collar and cuffs, light blue strip placed under the front buttons, white *chiripá* and white *calzoncillos*. The French Legion of Montevideo wore an elegant uniform with dark blue képi and blouse. On special occasions – especially on parade – the headgear was replaced by a dark blue shako having a brass front plate, red plume and yellow bottom band. The volunteers of the Basque Legion were uniformed exactly like the French legionaries, but with a red Carlist cap having dark blue bottom band and tassel. The Argentine Legion was dressed as follows: medium blue *bonnet de police* with red bottom band, white piping, white tassel and Argentine coat-of-arms embroidered in black on the front; medium blue blouse with red collar and cuffs piped in white, red pocket flaps and strip under the front buttons piped in white, white trousers and white belt equipment. The Italian Legion of Garibaldi was dressed with distinctive red blouses, the latter produced by using a stock of red cloth – bought for the butchers or "*saladeros*" of Buenos Aires – that was intercepted in Montevideo. Red soon became the distinctive colour of all the military units organized in his long career by Garibaldi. As an alternative to the round straw hat, a dark blue Carlist cap with black plume could be worn by the members of the Italian unit.

The four Uruguayan infantry battalions that were part of Urquiza's *Ejército Grande* were dressed with a French-style red uniform (see the relevant picture and caption). The "*Cazadores de la Unión*" Battalion formed after their disbandment

Uniforms of General Oribe's infantry, from left to right: officer, drum-major, officer and private. *Colour plate by Louis de Beaufort, part of the ASKB Military Collection.*

was uniformed as follows: dark blue képi with green bottom band and piping, dark blue blouse with green collar and cuffs, green pocket flaps and strip under the front buttons, dark blue trousers with green side-stripe and black belt equipment. The "*Voltijeros*" Battalion, instead, retained its red uniform. The artillery had dark blue shako with brass front plate and red falling plume, dark blue tunic with red collar, red piping to frontal plastron and pointed cuffs, dark blue trousers with red double side-stripe and black belt equipment. For the uniforms of the National Guard and of the Urban Company organized during 1858–1859, see the relevant pictures and captions. The two new infantry battalions organized after 1860 were dressed as follows: black shako with brass front plate and fittings, dark green bottom band and falling plume; dark blue single-breasted tunic with green piping to collar and cuffs, green piping to front, yellow "*sardinetas*" on collar and cuffs, dark blue trousers with green side-stripe and black belt equipment. The "Florida" Battalion raised by Flores had red shako with brass front plate, yellow side-chevron and dark green falling plume; dark blue tunic with red piping to front and round cuffs, dark green collar piped in red with yellow bugle horn badge, dark green epaulettes with yellow crescents, red trousers with dark green side-stripe and black belt equipment. The "*24 de Abril*" Battalion had dark blue shako with brass front plate, dark green side-chevron and red falling plume; dark blue tunic with red piping to front and pointed cuffs, dark green collar piped in red with yellow bugle horn badge, dark green epaulettes with red crescents, dark blue trousers with dark green side-stripe and black belt equipment. The uniforms of the Uruguayan Army at the time of the Paraguayan War were heavily influenced by those worn in the same years by the French Imperial Army of Napoleon III. The French influence had always been strong on Uruguayan military dress, since the establishment of the armed forces. No other country in South America had such a "European" aspect. However, there was no great uniformity among the various units. Due to the absence of official dress regulations, the majority of the officers were dressed with privately-purchased and non-regulation uniforms, which were sometimes quite extravagant. One of their common features was the profusion of buttons on the sleeves. At the beginning of the war, the Uruguayan soldiers marched to the front in their parade dress. As the war progressed, the ornate parade uniforms were soon replaced by much more comfortable campaign ones. The shako was abandoned, being replaced with the kepi, and entirely white summer uniforms came into use. Many Uruguayan soldiers who fought in the Allied Army wore a band on their headgear (over the national cockade), which was red, being embroidered in gold with laurel branches and the words "*EJERCITO ORIENTAL*".

Until after the Platine War in 1852, the Uruguayan Army had been mostly equipped with Brown Bess flintlock muskets. The Uruguayan government then began buying small numbers of new and much more modern weapons. These included Saint-Etienne percussion rifles M1854 and M1857, plus a certain number of Pattern 1853 Enfield rifles and carbines. In 1860 only the 1st "*Batallón de Cazadores*" was equipped with these new weapons. When the Paraguayan War broke out, the Uruguayan infantrymen were equipped with a mixture of firearms, percussion, flintlock, rifled and non-rifled weapons. For example, we know that two companies of the "*24 de Abril*" Battalion had flintlocks, while the rest of the unit was armed with percussion muskets. Shortly before its departure from Montevideo, the "Florida" Battalion had received Minié rifles, known in Uruguay as "Model n.1" rifles. On 24 October 1865, both the "Florida" and "*24 de Abril*" Battalions were re-equipped with new Minié rifles, of the so-called "Model n.2". As the war progressed, the whole Uruguayan Army was re-armed with Minié rifles of the "Model n.2". Officers were mostly armed with privately-purchased Lefaucheux handguns and French sabers.

Drum-major of General Oribe's infantry. *Colour plate by Francisco Ferrer Llul, part of the ASKB Military Collection.*

Cuirassier of General Oribe's cavalry. *Colour plate by Francisco Ferrer Llul, part of the ASKB Military Collection.*

Trooper of General Oribe's cavalry. *Colour plate by Louis de Beaufort, part of the ASKB Military Collection.*

Trooper of General Oribe's cavalry. *Colour plate by Louis de Beaufort, part of the ASKB Military Collection.*

Gaucho of General Oribe's cavalry. *Colour plate by Francisco Ferrer Llul, part of the ASKB Military Collection.*

NCO of General Rivera's regular infantry. *Colour plate by Francisco Ferrer Llul, part of the ASKB Military Collection.*

Private (left) and drummer (right) of the 4th Infantry Battalion of General Rivera's army. *Colour plate by Louis de Beaufort, part of the ASKB Military Collection.*

Officer of the *"Extramuros"* Battalion of General Rivera's army. *Colour plate by Francisco Ferrer Llul, part of the ASKB Military Collection.*

Trooper of Rivera's Squadron of Black Lancers. *Colour plate by Francisco Ferrer Llul, part of the ASKB Military Collection.*

Trooper of Rivera's Squadron of Black Lancers. *Colour plate by Louis de Beaufort, part of the ASKB Military Collection.*

Troopers of Rivera's Squadron of White Cuirassiers. *Colour plate by Louis de Beaufort, part of the ASKB Military Collection.*

Officer of Rivera's Squadron of White Lancers. *Colour plate by Louis de Beaufort, part of the ASKB Military Collection.*

Trooper of General Rivera's cavalry. *Colour plate by Francisco Ferrer Llul, part of the ASKB Military Collection.*

Trooper of General Rivera's cavalry. *Colour plate by Francisco Ferrer Llul, part of the ASKB Military Collection.*

Gaucho of General Rivera's cavalry. *Colour plate by Francisco Ferrer Llul, part of the ASKB Military Collection.*

Gunner (left) and officer (right) of General Rivera's artillery. The Highland bonnet worn by the gunner was one of those left in Montevideo by the British 73rd Regiment of Foot (which served for some months in the Uruguayan capital during 1845). *Colour plate by Francisco Ferrer Llul, part of the ASKB Military Collection.*

Uniforms of Rivera's French Legion, from left to right: officer in parade dress, officer in campaign dress and private in campaign dress. *Colour plate by Louis de Beaufort, part of the ASKB Military Collection.*

Below, left: Private of Rivera's Basque Legion. *Colour plate by Francisco Ferrer Llul, part of the ASKB Military Collection.*

Below, right: Private of Rivera's Italian Legion. *Colour plate by Francisco Ferrer Llul, part of the ASKB Military Collection.*

Uruguayan private (left) and officer (right) of the *"Voltijeros"* Battalion in 1852. *Colour plate by Louis de Beaufort, part of the ASKB Military Collection.*

Uniforms of the Uruguayan National Guard in 1858, from left to right: infantry officer in parade dress, infantryman in campaign dress and cavalryman in parade dress. *Colour plate by Louis de Beaufort, part of the ASKB Military Collection.*

Officer (left) and NCO (right) of Montevideo's Urban Company in 1859. *Colour plate by Louis de Beaufort, part of the ASKB Military Collection.*

The Paraguayan Army

History and organization

Soon after proclaiming their autonomy from Spain the Paraguayans organized their new military forces, which had to be created almost from zero since no regular Spanish colonial units had been previously deployed on their territory, except for a small corps of light infantry acting as the guard of the governor. The armed forces of the new nation were to comprise 1 battalion of infantry (with one grenadier company and four fusilier companies), 2 regiments of cavalry and 2 companies of artillery (one of which was made up of free blacks). The two mounted units were inherited from the colonial military organization and were two militia corps made up of Guaraní indians. The latter represented the majority of the Paraguayan population and were famous for their riding skills. They were accustomed to fight as light cavalrymen armed with spears and "*boleadoras*". In 1813, after Paraguay became a republic ruled by two consuls, a second infantry battalion was created so that each of the two consuls could have had the same number of military units under his command (one battalion of infantry, one regiment of cavalry and one company of artillery).

After becoming dictator of Paraguay in 1814, Francia soon organized two "guard" corps for his personal protection: a Battalion of Mounted Grenadiers with four companies and a Squadron of Lancers (all free blacks) with three companies. In March 1819 Francia disbanded the two cavalry regiments (named "*Costa Arriba*" and "*Costa Abajo*" after the areas of Paraguay where they were recruited) fearing that their officers could revolt against his new regime. For the same reason no officer of the Paraguayan Army was given a large command by Francia and the military law prescribed mandatory early retirement. Officers were rotated between units on a regular basis and the highest rank they could aspire to was that of captain. After Francia's death, in 1841, a new consular government was formed. This did not alter the existing structure of the Paraguayan Army.

The Paraguayan Army of 1845–1865

One year after becoming the new dictator of Paraguay, in 1845, Carlos Antonio López completely reorganized the Paraguayan military forces, anticipating a future confrontation with Rosas' Argentina. First of all, on 26 August 1845, he disbanded the general militia inherited from the colonial period (which had been much neglected by Francia) and replaced it with a new National Guard that would comprise all able-bodied male citizens aged 16–55. The new corps would be made up of infantry battalions with 4-7 companies each, cavalry regiments with 4-7 squadrons each and artillery corps with 3 companies each. Carlos Antonio López greatly expanded the Paraguayan regular forces, reorganizing the army into the following units: 4 battalions of line infantry with six companies each, 6 battalions of light infantry with six companies each, 4 regiments of cavalry with six companies each and 2 artillery corps with four companies/batteries each. During the last months of 1845 the Paraguayans mobilized their military forces and sent 5,000 of their best soldiers to fight against Rosas as allies of the Argentine Corrientes Province. Command of this "expeditionary

Paraguayan infantryman in 1845. *Colour plate by Francisco Ferrer Llul, part of the ASKB Military Collection.*

army" was given to the son of the Paraguayan dictator, the young Francisco Solano López. The troops were reorganized at his orders as four infantry battalions with six companies each, four cavalry regiments with six companies each and one artillery corps with two companies.

In 1850, under the guidance of some Brazilian instructors, the artillery of the Paraguayan Army was re-structured as one Battalion of Foot Artillery with four batteries and one Regiment of Horse Artillery with four batteries. In addition, the first two battalions of line infantry were given one attached artillery company each. Carlos Antonio López, like his predecessor, had a personal mounted bodyguard. This, organized in 1844, consisted of a single Squadron of Mounted Grenadiers with two companies. In 1855 this was expanded to become a regiment with four squadrons and named "*Acá Carayá*" or "Monkey Head" Regiment, since its members wore helmets trimmed with a tail of monkey fur. In 1845, while campaigning in Corrientes, Francisco Solano López organized his own mounted bodyguard by assembling the best elements of the cavalry regiments that were under his command into an elite Squadron of Dragoons with two companies. In 1851 this was expanded to become a regiment with four squadrons; the latter was named "*Acá Verá*" or "Golden Head" Regiment since its members wore shakos decorated with a band of golden bronze. Both the "*Acá Carayá*" and "*Acá Verá*" were to act as presidential guard. All their members were armed with carbines and not with lances like the other Paraguayan cavalrymen.

By 1864, two years after becoming president, Francisco Solano López had re-structured the Paraguayan Army into the following units: 7 infantry battalions with six companies each (five of fusiliers and one of "*cazadores*"), 5 cavalry regiments with four squadrons each (a single squadron mustered two companies), 1 battalion of foot artillery with four companies/batteries, 2 regiments of horse artillery with four companies/batteries each and 1 naval infantry battalion with six companies. The latter unit was numbered as the 1st Infantry Battalion of the Paraguayan Army and was considered to be an elite corps. The soldiers of the 6th Infantry Battalion and of the 7th Infantry Battalion were trained to act as "*zapadores*" (sappers) if needed.

Due to the Brazilian military intervention in the Uruguayan War, Francisco Solano López decided to build a massive military encampment along the border with Brazil. In March 1864 he mobilized all the able-bodied male citizens aged 16–55 and ordered the construction of the Cerro León encampment, where one infantry battalion and one cavalry regiment would train the new recruits in order to form new military units. By December 1864 the Paraguayan Army had completed its planned expansion and included the following corps: 30 infantry battalions, 23 cavalry regiments, 2 artillery regiments and 1 naval infantry battalion (including a company of naval artillery). In a few months Francisco Solano López had transformed the Paraguayan Army into the largest military force of South America. Each of the infantry battalions had four fusilier companies and two light companies; each of the cavalry regiments had four squadrons. The two artillery regiments had four companies/batteries each; one was of foot artillery and the other of horse artillery. Four of the senior infantry battalions – those numbered 2-5 that already existed before 1864 – were given new muskets recently bought from Europe. The 2nd Battalion was given percussion smoothbores and was re-named "*Cazadores de la Guardia*" Battalion; the other three were given percussion rifles and were re-named "*Rifleros*" Battalions. By March 1865 a further 8 infantry battalions, 6 cavalry regiments and 2 horse artillery regiments were mobilized. With the inclusion of all the able-bodied men into the regular army, the National Guard practically disappeared.

Paraguayan infantry officer, dressed with 1848 parade uniform. *Colour plate by Francisco Ferrer Llul, part of the ASKB Military Collection.*

Uniforms and weapons

During the period 1811–1842 the uniform of the Paraguayan infantry and artillery consisted of black round hat with national cockade, dark blue single-breasted jacket with red collar and round cuffs, white trousers and white belt equipment. The cavalry was uniformed quite similarly, but with white cords on the left shoulder. Sometimes the mounted soldiers replaced the black round hat with a simple brown busby made of fur. The elite Squadron of Lancers, entirely made up of black soldiers, wore a distinctive white uniform. The Battalion of Mounted Grenadiers was dressed in the same way but with reversed colours (red jacket worn over a white waistcoat). In 1842 the standard headgear of the Paraguayan Army became a dark blue *gorrete* with red piping and tassel, but the rest of the existing uniforms did not change. In 1844 the uniform of the Mounted Grenadiers became as follows: red *gorrete* with double piping in dark green and in black, dark green jacket with black collar and cuffs, three golden "*sardinetas*" on collar and cuffs, dark green trousers with black side-stripe.

On 27 April 1848 the first official dress regulations of the Paraguayan Army were promulgated which remained valid until 1876, but detailed only the uniforms of officers. The latter were completely different from those of rankers, being clearly influenced by the contemporary models of Napoleon III's French Army. The dress regulations of 1848 abandoned the previous Spanish style for uniforms and rank insignia, introducing a new one based on the French model. Many jackets or tailcoats of the Paraguayan officers were even made in France. The parade uniform for all officers' ranks was a dark blue tailcoat with red collar and cuffs, worn over a blue or white waistcoat (the white one was for summer), with gold lace embroidery on collar and cuffs. Also trousers were blue or white, depending on season, with red side stripes (golden for generals). Officers were authorized to wear sashes (usually tricolour ones) without tassels but with little knots. The headgear was a French-style shako with the gilded Paraguayan coat of arms on the front. It also had a falling plume in the national colours of Paraguay. On parade, cocked hats with tricolour plumes were in common use. Non-regulation hussar-style uniforms were sometimes used by cavalry officers both on parade or on campaign. In the field, infantry and foot artillery officers had a much simpler dress, with dark blue or red kepi with gold rank lace and quarter-piping, dark blue single-breasted frock-coat with red collar and cuffs, gilt buttons (including four at the rear seam of the sleeves) and shoulder bars, simple red sash worn around the waist and blue or white trousers (depending on season). Later in the war, officers started to use the same red blouses as the common soldiers on campaign, being distinguishable from their men only by the use of boots and kepi, which were both forbidden for rankers. For more details on the M1848 uniforms for officers, see the relevant pictures and captions.

In 1855 the Mounted Grenadiers were expanded to become a regiment and received the new denomination of "Monkey Head" Regiment, together with a new uniform. The latter was as follows: crude leather helmet with bronze reinforcements and black peak, having a monkey's tail added as a crest and long black horsehair hanging on the soldier's back. Enamel bars were placed on each side of the helmet, painted in different colours. The tunic was red, with white collar, pointed cuffs and frontal plastron. White trousers were worn over black leather grenadier boots. The "Monkey Head" Regiment, as Presidential Escort, was the only unit to have the privilege of wearing boots. The "Golden Head" Regiment was given a new uniform in 1851. Until then the elite Squadron of Dragoons was uniformed as the rest of the Paraguayan cavalry, as follows: tall black shako having no decorations but top and bottom bands in gold lace; red blouse with black collar, cuffs, shoulder patches, front placket strip and upwards-pointing pocket flaps. White trousers worn under a short striped "*chiripá*" and brown leather apron (called "*culera*") having red fringes.

After Francisco Solano López assumed power the uniforms of the Paraguayan military forces were rapidly changed, albeit without the promulgation of any official dress regulations. The *gorrete* introduced in 1842 was replaced with a black shako, having three bands in the national colours of Paraguay painted around its base. The shakos of infantry and artillery had a simple national cockade on the front, while those of cavalry had a "fleur-de-lys" badge painted in the national colours of Paraguay. As an alternative to the shako, a red *bonnet de police* with black bottom band and white piping could be worn. The dark blue jacket was replaced by a red blouse, hav-

Paraguayan infantry officer, dressed with 1848 campaign uniform. *Colour plate by Francisco Ferrer Llul, part of the ASKB Military Collection.*

ing the following elements in black: collar, cuffs, pocket flaps and strip placed under the front buttons. The naval infantry was the only corps to have the blouse in black with red facings; its shako bore the inscription "*REPUBLICA O MUERTE ESCUADRA NACIONAL*". The universal blouse was worn with white trousers by the infantry/foot artillery; the cavalry/horse artillery used it with striped *chiripá* and white *calzoncillos* (see the relevant pictures and captions for more details). The usual dress of a Paraguayan male consisted of a tall hat made of straw, a white shirt with embroidered front and cuffs and white fringed trousers called "*calzoncillos cribados*", worn under a striped kilt (the "*chiripá*"). Many Paraguayans did not use shoes and, when mounted, they wore iron spurs tied on their bare feet. This national dress was the base for the uniforms used during the conflict of 1864–1870. When serving in the army, the Paraguayan men simply wore a red blouse over their civilian dress and substituted the straw hat with a shako. The blouse was made of wool and had black (rarely dark blue) collar and cuffs. The shirt, underwear and pantaloons were all made of white linen or cotton. The blouse, or "*camiseta*", was of red wool with black collar, cuffs and front placket strip under the buttons. The Paraguayan shako was crudely made in hard black leather with a visor. The shape of it varied between the branches of service, but all were painted with a band in the Paraguayan national colours. The infantry ones were shorter and had the national cockade (red-white-blue) painted on the front. The uniforms of corporals and sergeants had no peculiar features. Sticks were used as both a rank distinction and a punishment tool. The lightweight white trousers could be simple or have some fringes on the cuffs. However, the "*calzoncillos*" were frequently replaced by the much more comfortable "*chiripá*" (a very common practice also for cavalry). All the belts of the equipment were white. Some cavalrymen simply wore the Paraguayan national dress, with white shirts or blouses and "*calzoncillos*". However, simple red shirts or blouses were much more common. The striped "*chiripá*" was of universal use among the cavalrymen, because of its great comfort while riding. However, some soldiers preferred white loose pantaloons instead of the kilt. "Ponchos" worn wrapped around the waist were very popular, also because they gave some protection against enemy bullets. The cavalry shako was taller than that of the infantry and had a peculiar badge painted on the front, over the band in national colours. It was a cockade having a flower shape, very similar to a "fleur de lys", and frequently it had a gilded button in the centre. The cavalry troops were mounted in a local fashion known as "*recado*" (country saddle), without reins or bridles but using only a rope passed through the horse's mouth. All cavalrymen wore enormous spurs called "*nazarenas*". The light artillery was dressed and equipped like cavalry, while the heavy artillery soldiers had the same uniforms as the infantry. Both mounted and foot artillery used the infantry shako, with the cockade in

Uniforms of the Paraguayan infantry in 1865, from left to right: private, NCO, private and officer. The first figure has a black shako with three painted bands in the colours of Paraguay around its base and a striped *chiripá* worn over the shoulders. The NCO has a red blouse, a brown leather apron worn over the *chiripá* and a typical Guaraní whip. The veteran private has only the standard shako with painted bands and the striped *chiripá*. The officer wears a wide-brimmed straw hat, a red blouse and extremely tall brown leather boots.

national colours. The blouses of the heavy artillery had black piping to the pocket flaps. Horse artillery wore the "*chiripá*" under the leather apron, foot artillery had only the "*culera*". The Paraguayan militia used the same uniforms as the regular army, with foot troops dressed like the infantry, mounted ones like the cavalry. The only difference was in the shako: all the militiamen had one with a peculiar painted badge in national colours. This was very simple, consisting of three vertical lines which were supposed to represent three feathers. Obviously, pieces of civilian dress were frequently worn and white trousers were rarely used, being replaced by the more comfortable "*chiripá*". Striped sashes and "ponchos" were very common, worn together with simple red shirts or blouses.

The Paraguayan Army's weapons were mostly antique, obsolete and in poor repair due to many years of use. The standard infantry weapons were the old Brown Bess flintlock muskets, of which 20,000 were bought (mainly from Brazil) during 1845–1850 and then distributed to the soldiers gathered at Cerro León in 1864. Only three infantry battalions were given Witton or Enfield percussion rifles in 1863. All muskets and rifles had a French-made knife-bayonet, which was always mounted. The 6th Infantry Battalion was also armed with cutlasses, which had been seized from Argentine steamships captured during the attack against Corrientes. Thanks to these new weapons, this unit started to act as a naval infantry battalion. Cavalrymen were usually armed with lances three yards long and sabers. Flintlock carbines were very rare and issued only to some regiments. The "*Acá Carayá*" and "*Acá Verá*" were armed with Turner rifled carbines (the name refers not to a manufacturer, but to a rare class of US weapons made by German gunsmiths). Many of the sabers were of the old stirrup-hilted British Pattern 1796 for light cavalry or local copies of it. The "*bolas*", used to entangle the legs of enemy horses, were very common in the Paraguayan mounted units.

Paraguayan trooper of the "*Monkey Head*" Cavalry Regiment. *Colour plate by Francisco Ferrer Llul, part of the ASKB Military Collection.*

Paraguayan trooper of the *"Golden Head"* Cavalry Regiment. *Colour plate by Francisco Ferrer Llul, part of the ASKB Military Collection.*

Paraguayan cavalry NCO in 1870. *Colour plate by Francisco Ferrer Llul, part of the ASKB Military Collection.*

Paraguayan cavalryman in 1865. *Colour plate by Francisco Ferrer Llul, part of the ASKB Military Collection.*

The Peruvian Army

History and organization

During the Spanish colonial period Peru was garrisoned by a large number of regular military units, which were supported by many locally-raised militia corps. These remained loyal to the Spaniards during South America's Wars of Independence and thus formed the core of the "loyalist" troops that fought against the patriot insurgents. Peru was the military stronghold of Spain in South America and one of the richest regions of the Spanish colonial empire. It was from Peru, in fact, that the Spanish/Loyalist troops marched against the Argentine patriots in the south and against the Gran Colombian ones in the north. In 1820 José de San Martín, the military leader of the Argentine patriots, led an amphibious expedition against the Spanish positions in Peru. He landed on the latter's coastline at the head of a joint Argentine-Chilean army and soon started to be supported by the local population. After having obtained some early victories over the Spaniards, the Argentine general decided to channel the enthusiasm of the Peruvian volunteers who were joining his forces in order to form some locally-raised military corps. These included the following units: "*Auxiliares de Ica*" (a cavalry squadron with three companies), "*Cazadores del Ejército*" (a light infantry battalion), "*Veteranos de Jauja*" (a line infantry battalion) and "Hussars of the Escort" (a cavalry squadron). On 20 February 1821 San Martín decided to assemble the first three corps into a "Peruvian Division", which was to be commanded by Agustín Gamarra. The latter was the most important military commander of the Peruvian patriots, who had previously served as an officer in the Spanish colonial military corps. The "*Auxiliaries de Ica*" received the new denomination of "*Granaderos a Caballo del Perù*" and the "*Veteranos de Jauja*" became the "*Leales del Perù*". The latter mustered six companies and, after marching on the Peruvian capital of Lima, were re-named "*Cazadores del Perù*".

During 1821 San Martín expanded the Peruvian military forces, by ordering the formation of a new mixed corps that would be known as "Peruvian Legion". This consisted of one line infantry battalion, two squadrons of hussars (one of which was the former "Hussars of the Escort") and one company of mounted artillery equipped with light guns. Following the liberation of large areas of Peru, the patriots could organize more military corps: one infantry battalion in Ica, one infantry battalion in Trujillo, one infantry battalion in Piura, one squadron of lancers and one squadron of mounted chasseurs. In January 1822 San Martín decided to give a proper organization to the newly-born Peruvian Army, by giving progressive numbers and new denominations to the existing corps. The "*Cazadores del Perù*" became the 1st Line Infantry Battalion, the "Trujillo Battalion" became the 2nd Line Infantry Battalion, the "Ica Battalion" became the 3rd Line Infantry Battalion, the "Piura Battalion" became the 4th Line Infantry Battalion. A new squadron of dragoons and a small engineer corps were also formed. Following

Peruvian infantryman (left) and cavalryman (right) wearing 1825 uniform. *Colour plate by Patricio Greve Moller, copyright of Gabriele Esposito.*

the creation of the Peruvian Congress, San Martín decided to leave Peru in the last months of 1822, despite not having expelled the Spaniards from the whole of Peruvian territory.

In 1823 the first Constitution of Peru was promulgated, according to which the first Peruvian "national" army was raised. The new military forces were formed around the elite Peruvian Legion, which had performed extremely well against the Spaniards. The infantry battalion of the Peruvian Legion was transformed into a regiment with two battalions, while the two hussar squadrons of the Peruvian Legion were expanded to become a regiment with four squadrons. Two new line infantry battalions were added to the existing ones. Command of the new Peruvian Army was assigned to Andrés de Santa Cruz, an experienced officer who had already served in the Spanish colonial forces before becoming an important patriot leader.

Santa Cruz transformed the 1st Line Infantry Battalion into a regiment with two battalions and gave new denominations to the two line infantry battalions that had recently been formed (which became the 5th Line Infantry Battalion and 6th Line Infantry Battalion). He also improved the training and discipline of the Peruvian troops, for example by organizing the first military academy of Peru. Since 1821 the Peruvian military forces included a battalion of naval infantry, which was soon expanded to become a "brigade" mustering two battalions. By the half of 1823 the Peruvian Army comprised the following units: two line infantry regiments having two battalions each, five line infantry battalions numbered 2-6, one light infantry battalion ("*Cazadores del Ejército*"), one regiment of hussars, one squadron of lancers, one squadron of dragoons and one brigade of artillery. During 1823 the military forces of Gran Colombia, commanded by Simón Bolívar, entered the territory of Peru in order to continue the struggle against the Spanish troops that were still deployed in South America. The expansion of the Peruvian military forces continued, with the formation of the following new corps: the 7th Line Infantry Battalion, the "*Regimiento de Tiradores*" (a light infantry unit with two battalions), one regiment of cuirassiers, one squadron of lancers and one squadron of hussars. After entering Lima, in the last months of 1823, Simón Bolívar decided to re-structure the Peruvian Army and to reduce its numerical consistency in a significant way. As a result, the Peruvian military forces came to comprise the following corps: four battalions of line infantry, one regiment of cavalry and one company of artillery. All the units existing previously were disbanded and their members were absorbed into the Gran Colombian Army. Of the four new line infantry battalions one was known as the Peruvian Legion, while the others were numbered 1-3. The single cavalry unit was a hussar regiment with three squadrons, while the single artillery company was equipped with six mountain guns. On 6 August 1824, at the important Battle of Junín, the Peruvian hussar regiment distinguished itself and won the day for Bolívar. The latter, to reward the unit, changed its denomination from "Peruvian Hussars" to "Junín Hussars". On 9 December 1824, at the decisive Battle of

Peruvian grenadier (left) and cavalryman (right) of the Guard Division wearing 1827 uniform.
Colour plate by Patricio Greve Moller, copyright of Gabriele Esposito.

Peruvian infantryman (left) and cavalryman (right) wearing 1828 uniform. *Colour plate by Patricio Greve Moller, copyright of Gabriele Esposito.*

Peruvian fusilier of the 1st "Ayacucho" Battalion (left) and cazador of the 1st "Callao" Battalion (right) wearing 1830 uniform. *Colour plate by Patricio Greve Moller, copyright of Gabriele Esposito.*

Ayacucho, the multi-national patriot army of Bolívar (which comprised Gran Colombian and Peruvian troops as well as one Argentine cavalry squadron) defeated in a decisive way the last Spanish military forces stationed on South America's mainland. The Wars of Independence were now over and thus the Gran Colombian troops abandoned the Peruvian territory. At the same time, during 1825, the Peruvian Army was completely reorganized and significantly expanded.

According to the new structure introduced in 1825, the Peruvian Army's infantry was to be organized in regiments having two battalions each. A single battalion was to muster one company of grenadiers, one company of *cazadores* and six companies of fusiliers. Three such new regiments were created: the "Ayacucho" Line Infantry Regiment, the "Pichincha" Line Infantry Regiment and the "Callao" Line Infantry Regiment. The cavalry was to consist of two regiments with four squadrons each, the "Junín Hussars" and the "Dragoons of Peru". The latter corps was later re-named as the "Lanceros del Callao". The artillery was to be organized as a single brigade with three foot companies and one mounted company. The engineers, as previously, continued to consist of just a few officers having specific technical skills. In 1827 the new organization of the infantry based on regiments was abandoned and thus the Peruvian foot troops were reorganized as six independent battalions: 1st *Ayacucho*, 2nd *Ayacucho*, 1st *Callao*, 2nd *Callao*, 1st *Pichincha* and 2nd *Pichincha*. The first four were assembled together in order to form the 1st Division of the Peruvian Army, which was also known as the "Guard Division" since it was under the direct control of the government. The remaining two formed the 2nd Division of the Peruvian Army. The cavalry continued to consist of two regiments, the "Junín Hussars" and the "Lanceros del Callao". The first was attached to the "Guard Division" and thus had elite status, while the second was attached to the 2nd Division. The artillery brigade was expanded in order to comprise five foot companies and one mounted company. The infantry battalions had eight companies each as previously, one of grenadiers, one of *cazadores* and six of fusiliers. A company of sappers was added to each battalion in time of war. The cavalry regiments had three squadrons with two companies each, plus one independent company of "tira-

dores" armed with flintlock carbines. During 1827, following the beginning of the hostilities with Gran Colombia, two new infantry battalions were raised: the 1st *Zepita* and the 2nd *Zepita*.

In 1829 Gamarra, as the new President of Peru, introduced a new general structure for the Peruvian military forces. The "Guard Division" was disbanded and the existing eight line infantry battalions were re-structured in four divisions. A ninth line infantry battalion was raised. The cavalry was expanded to comprise four regiments, each of which was attached to one division of the Peruvian Army. The "Junín Hussars" retained their denomination, while the "Lanceros del Callao" were renamed "Granaderos del Callao". The two new cavalry regiments formed in 1829 were known as "Dragones de Arequipa" and "Lanceros del Cuzco". As a result of the above changes, in 1829, this was the internal composition of the Peruvian Army's four divisions:

- **1st Division:** 1st *Pichincha* Battalion, 1st *Zepita* Battalion, 2nd *Ayacucho* Battalion and "Dragones de Arequipa" Regiment;
- **2nd Division:** 2nd *Pichincha* Battalion, 2nd *Callao* Battalion and "Junín Hussars" Regiment;
- **3rd Division:** 2nd *Zepita* Battalion, 9th Line Infantry Battalion and "Granaderos del Callao" Regiment;
- **4th Division:** 1st *Ayacucho* Battalion, 1st *Callao* Battalion and "Lanceros del Cuzco" Regiment.

In the last months of 1834 the Peruvian Army was reorganized again and significantly reduced in its numbers. The infantry was re-structured in six independent battalions, each of which comprised eight companies (one of grenadiers, one of *cazadores* and six of fusiliers). The cavalry, instead, was re-structured in one regiment and three independent squadrons. The six infantry battalions had the following official denominations: 1st Battalion "Pichincha", 2nd Battalion "Peruvian Legion", 3rd Battalion "Defensores de la Libertad", 4th Battalion "Cazadores del Rímac", 5th Battalion "Ayacucho" and 6th Battalion "Maquinhuayo". The cavalry corps were the following: "Junín Hussars" Regiment, "Lanceros de Arequipa" Squadron, "Cazadores de la Libertad" Squadron and "Guías" Squadron. The artillery continued to be organized as a single brigade, having four foot companies and one mounted company. The new general structure introduced in 1834 remained unchanged until 1847, suffering no modifications during the turbulent period of the Peru-Bolivian Confederation (1836–1839). In 1838 the "brigade" of naval infantry, which had been progressively reduced from two battalions to two companies, was disbanded and its members were absorbed into

Peruvian trooper of the *"Junín Hussars"* Regiment (left) and trooper of the *"Granaderos del Callao"* Regiment (right) wearing 1830 uniform. *Colour plate by Patricio Greve Moller, copyright of Gabriele Esposito.*

the "*Pichincha*" Battalion. In 1840 the Peruvian marines were re-formed as a single battalion.

In 1847 the sapper company formed in each infantry battalion in time of war was disbanded and the cavalry was consolidated in three regiments, each of the latter assigned to an elite company of "*flanqueadores*" armed with carbines. The "*tiradores*" company of the "Junín Hussars" Regiment was dissolved. The artillery was re-structured as a brigade having one foot battalion (with four companies) and one mounted squadron (with two companies). The naval infantry was re-structured as a battalion with six companies. In 1848 the number of fusilier companies in each line infantry battalion was reduced to four and the number of squadrons in each cavalry regiment was reduced to two. The artillery was reorganized into three foot companies and one mounted company. All the units received new official denominations, according to the list that follows: 1st Battalion "*Pichincha*", 2nd Battalion "*Zepita*", 3rd Battalion "*Callao*", 4th Battalion "*Junín*", 5th Battalion "*Ayacucho*", 6th Battalion "*Yungay*", 1st Regiment "Junín Hussars", 2nd Regiment "*Lanceros de Torata*" and 3rd Regiment "*Lanceros de la Escolta*". The latter corps was tasked with acting as the mounted bodyguard of the president. In time of peace the six infantry battalions were assembled into three brigades; in time of war they were transformed into regiments having two battalions each and the three brigades were transformed into divisions. In 1855 the naval infantry was expanded and became a "brigade" having two battalions; the latter existed until 1870, when they were disbanded and their members were absorbed into the line infantry.

In 1856, after a period of internal unrest that very badly affected the Peruvian military forces, the Peruvian Army was reorganized. The infantry was expanded and came to comprise eight battalions, while the cavalry retained its usual composition. The artillery came to comprise one foot battalion with

Peruvian trooper of the "*Dragones de Arequipa*" Regiment (left) and trooper of the "*Lanceros del Cuzco*" Regiment (right) wearing 1830 uniform. *Colour plate by Patricio Greve Moller, copyright of Gabriele Esposito.*

Peruvian infantryman wearing 1835 uniform. *Colour plate by Patricio Greve Moller, copyright of Gabriele Esposito.*

four companies and one mounted squadron. In 1858, following the outbreak of hostilities with Ecuador, the infantry was expanded to comprise 12 battalions, assembled into three divisions having four battalions each. The three existing cavalry units were supplemented by a new regiment and by a squadron of cuirassiers, which was tasked with acting as the mounted bodyguard of the president. On 18 September 1859 a new infantry unit, the "*Cazadores del Rímac*" Column, was formed from volunteers for the war against Ecuador. The corps, consisting of just two companies, was disbanded in 1860.

After the end of the hostilities with Ecuador, the Peruvian government decided to not de-mobilize its military forces and thus the composition of the Peruvian Army suffered no alterations. In 1865 the number of infantry battalions was reduced to ten, which were assembled into five divisions having two battalions each. The cavalry came to comprise just three regiments, which made up a single mounted division. In 1867, following the end of the Chincha Islands War with Spain, the Peruvian infantry was reduced to eight battalions that made up four divisions. The artillery was re-structured as one regiment of fortress artillery equipped with positional guns, two battalions of field artillery equipped with mountain guns and one squadron of mounted artillery equipped with light guns. In 1867 the few engineer officers started to be supplemented with a brigade of sappers, who acted as their labour force. The new organization described above remained unchanged until 1872,

---

Peruvian trooper of the "*Lanceros de Arequipa*" Squadron (left) and trooper of the "*Cazadores de la Libertad*" Squadron (right). *Colour plate by Patricio Greve Moller, copyright of Gabriele Esposito.*

when the infantry was re-structured in 11 battalions having six companies each (the elite companies of grenadiers and *cazadores* were disbanded). The cavalry continued to muster three regiments, having two active squadrons and one reserve squadron each. The artillery was reorganized as one field regiment and one fortress regiment with two brigades each; a single artillery brigade mustered four companies/batteries. In addition to the above, there were one company of artillery train and one company of sappers.

Uniforms and weapons

The dress regulations promulgated in 1825 introduced elegant Napoleonic-style uniforms for the Peruvian Army, which were clearly influenced by the Spanish Army's dress regulations of 1815. The infantry wore a black shako with national cockade, red cord and coloured plume (half green and half yellow) together with a dark blue coatee having red standing collar, round cuffs and shoulder straps. Both the facings and the frontal plastron of the coatee were piped in yellow. Trousers were white. The cavalry was dressed with black shako having national cockade, red pompom and white decorative cord together with dark blue coatee having green piping to facings and frontal plastron. Trousers were white. The artillery was uniformed similarly to the infantry, but with the following peculiar elements: red plume and brass badge on the shako (consisting of two crossed cannons), yellow flaming grenades on the collar and turnbacks of the coatee, dark blue shoulder straps piped in red. The Guard Division created in 1827 was assigned peculiar red uniforms. The infantry wore a red coatee with light blue standing collar and round cuffs piped in yellow, the frontal plastron and the shoulder straps had yellow piping. Grenadiers, as shown in one of the colour figures, wore a black bearskin and red epaulettes on the shoulders; *cazadores* had a black shako (with green short plume and decorative cord) and green epaulettes on the shoulders. The shako of fusiliers had white cord and pompom in the two national colours of Peru. Trousers were white for all the infantry companies. The cavalry of the Guard Division was dressed as follows: black busby with red cloth bag, short plume and decorative cord; red coatee with yellow piping to light blue standing collar and pointed cuffs, yellow badge embroidered on the collar (crossed laurel branches), yellow piping to frontal plastron, brass "contre-epaulettes" and white trousers. In 1827 the uniform of the line infantry was simplified and became that shown in one of the colour pictures: black shako with national cockade, white cord, red pompom and brass badge bearing unit number; dark blue single-breasted coatee with red standing collar and round cuffs piped in white, red frontal piping, dark blue shoulder straps and brass unit number on collar; dark blue trousers with red side-stripe. The artillery was dressed very similarly to the infantry, but with two differences: yellow flaming grenade on each side of the collar and red cord of the shako. The line cavalry was assigned a lancer-style "Polish" uniform, comprising "*czapka*" headgear; this dress is shown in one of the colour pictures.

Peruvian infantryman wearing 1839 uniform. *Colour plate by Patricio Greve Moller, copyright of Gabriele Esposito.*

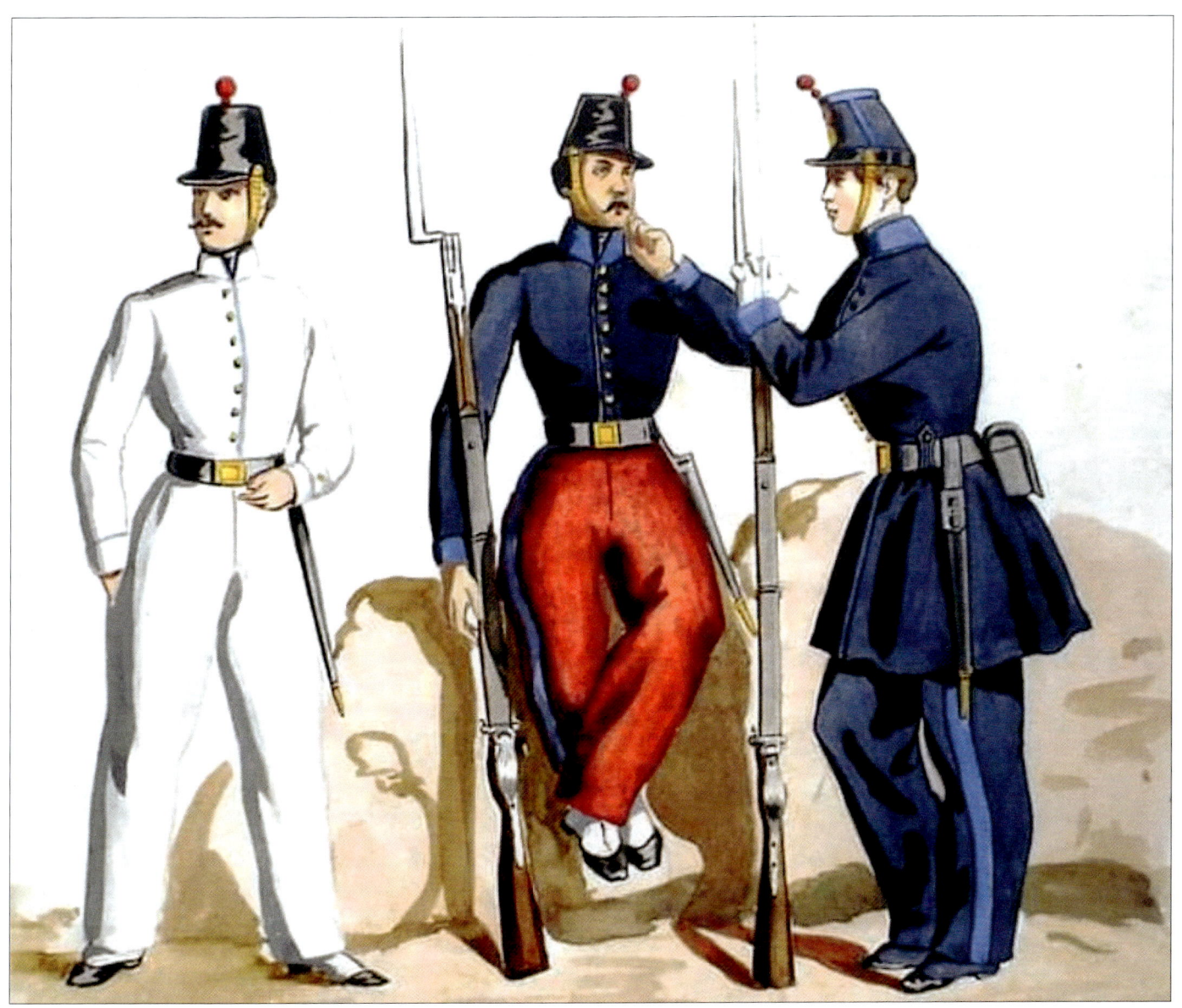

Peruvian infantrymen wearing 1852 uniform. The figure on the left wears white fatigue dress, the figure on the right wears the trousers used with service dress. *Photo courtesy of Patricio Greve Moller.*

In 1830 new dress regulations were promulgated, according to which each infantry battalion was to wear a distinctive uniform. The black shako had yellow pompom, national cockade, yellow decorative cord and brass badge bearing unit number for all the corps. The coatee was single-breasted with standing collar, round cuffs, cuff flaps and frontal piping; it was dark blue for some units and red for others. The facing colour was different for each corps; collar, cuffs and piping were in facing colour. Trousers were dark blue during cold months and white during hot months for all units. Grenadiers had red short plume and cord of the shako, yellow "*sardinetas*" on the cuffs and red epaulettes; *cazadores* had green short plume and cord of the shako, yellow "*sardinetas*" on the cuffs and green epaulettes. The units dressed with red coatee were the following: 1st *Ayacucho*, 1st *Pichincha*, 2nd *Ayacucho* and 2nd *Pichincha*. Each of the four cavalry regiments existing in 1830 had its own peculiar uniform, as shown in the relevant colour pictures. The "Junín Hussars" were dressed like hussars with red dolman and dark blue pelisse, the "*Granaderos del Callao*" were dressed like mounted chasseurs with red coatee having green facings and yellow frontal frogging, the "*Dragones de Arequipa*" were dressed like dragoons with black helmet and yellow coatee, the "*Lanceros del Cuzco*" had black shako and dark green coatee. The artillery was dressed exactly like the infantry, in dark blue with red facings. In 1832 the uniform of the "Junín Hussars" was slightly modified to cut costs. It now had light blue dolman and red pelisse. During 1835 new dress regulations were promulgated, which remained valid during the turbulent period of the Peru-Bolivian Confederation. These issued the following uniform to the infantry, which was identical for all the battalions: black shako with red top band and bottom band, national cockade, short plume in the national colours of Peru and brass badge bearing the Peruvian coat-of-arms; dark blue single-breasted coatee with red standing collar bearing brass unit number and red round cuffs having dark blue cuff flaps; white piping to front of the coatee, collar, cuffs and cuff flaps; red shoulder straps piped in white, dark blue trousers with white side-stripe during cold months and white trousers with red side-stripe during hot months. The uniforms of the artillery and of the "Junín Hussars" Regiment were not modified by the dress regulations of 1835, while each of the newly-formed cavalry corps received a peculiar uniform. The latter, as shown in the colour pictures, comprised black shako and single-breasted short-tailed coatee for all the three corps. The "*Lanceros de Arequipa*" Squadron had red coatee with dark blue facings, the "*Cazadores de la Libertad*" Squadron had dark blue coatee with red facings and the "*Guías*" Squadron had dark blue coatee with green facings.

After the dissolution of the Peru-Bolivian Confederation, in 1839, the Peruvian state experienced serious economic difficulties and thus the army had to be significantly reduced in its numbers. At the same time, new and much simpler uniforms were introduced. The infantry started to be dressed as follows: black shako with brass frontal plate bearing the Peruvian coat-of-arms, national cockade and light blue pompom; dark blue single-breasted coatee with light blue standing collar and round cuffs, dark blue cuff flaps, light blue piping to the front and dark blue shoulder straps piped in light blue. Trousers were entirely dark blue during cold months and entirely white during hot months. The uniform of the artillery was not modified and thus remained that prescribed in 1830; the cavalry, instead, was dressed like the infantry but with red as facing colour instead of light blue. The latter, starting with the dress regulations of 1839, became the distinctive colour of the Peruvian infantry. In 1852 the Peruvian government decided to change completely the uniforms of its military forces, replacing

---

Peruvian cavalrymen wearing 1852 uniform. The figure on the left wears white fatigue dress, the figure on the right wears the trousers used with service dress. *Photo courtesy of Patricio Greve Moller.*

the old-fashioned coatee with the tunic that was becoming extremely popular in Europe. As a result of the above, new dress regulations were promulgated that were based on the French ones of 1845. The uniform of the infantry became that shown in one of the colour pictures, with dark blue tunic having light blue facings and "*garance*" red trousers having light blue side-stripe. Also the shako was modelled on the contemporary French one. The cavalry was dressed similarly to the infantry, but with red falling plume and pompom on the shako as well as with red as facing colour. The trousers were "*garance*" red with dark blue side-stripe. The artillery was uniformed like the cavalry, but with two peculiarities: yellow flaming grenade on the collar and round cuffs instead of the cavalry's pointed ones (the latter were worn by the mounted artillery). The new cuirassier squadron of 1858 was dressed like the rest of the cavalry, but wore metal cuirasses painted in black (see the relevant colour picture). The "*Cazadores del Rímac*" of 1859 wore a peculiar uniform consisting of iron grey tunic with green facings and red trousers with green side-stripe.

In 1863 new dress regulations were promulgated, which continued to follow contemporary French military fashions. As shown in the colour pictures, the uniform of the infantry comprised dark blue tunic with light blue standing collar and round cuffs together with "*garance*" red trousers having light blue side-stripe. The cavalry had dark blue tunic with red standing collar and pointed cuffs together with "*garance*" red trousers having a black triple side-stripe. The headgear was a white metal helmet for one of the regiments (which was classified as "heavy cavalry") and a black shako for the other two (which were classified as "light cavalry"). The artillery was uniformed similarly to the infantry, but with the following four differences: brass unit badge on the shako consisting of two crossed cannons and one flaming grenade, yellow flaming grenade on collar, red facings and piping (instead of the infantry's light blue ones) and dark blue trousers with red side-stripe. During the whole period 1825–1865, the naval infantry was always dressed quite similarly to the line infantry except for having anchor badges embroidered on the collar.

With regard to weapons, until 1856 the Peruvian infantry was mostly equipped with Brown Bess flintlock muskets. From that year, however, it was re-equipped with new percussion muskets purchased in the USA. The latter were of the M1842 Springfield model and were bought thanks to the investment of significant sums of money. Following the outbreak of the Chincha Islands War, in 1865, the Peruvian government purchased thousands of Pattern 1853 Enfield muskets from Great Britain and replaced the M1842 Springfield weapons. Until the 1850s the Peruvian cavalry was mostly equipped with old-fashioned sabres of the British M1796 model for light cavalry. These were gradually replaced, as it happened in several other armies of South America, with sabres of the French M1822 model for light cavalry.

Peruvian artillerymen wearing 1852 uniform. The figure on the left is a foot artilleryman with service dress, the figure on the centre is a foot artilleryman with parade dress and the figure on the right is a horse artilleryman with parade dress. *Photo courtesy of Patricio Greve Moller.*

Peruvian infantryman of the "*Cazadores del Rímac*" in 1858. *Colour plate by Patricio Greve Moller, copyright of Gabriele Esposito.*

Peruvian trooper of the "*Cuirassiers of the Escort*" Squadron in 1858. *ASKB Military Collection.*

Opposite page: Peruvian infantryman (left) and cavalryman (right) wearing 1863 uniform. *Colour plate by Patricio Greve Moller, copyright of Gabriele Esposito.*

Peruvian infantry corporal (left) and artilleryman (right) wearing 1863 uniform. *ASKB Military Collection*.

The Chilean Army

History and organization

During 1817–1823, under the leadership of Bernardo O'Higgins, the Chilean Army was organized as a proper military institution and gained a lot of combat experience by fighting against the Spaniards in Peru. Together with the Argentine military forces of San Martín, in fact, the Chilean ones of O'Higgins made up the famous "*Ejército Unido Libertador del Perù*". In 1817, after the Spaniards had temporarily reconquered part of Chile, the Chilean military forces were completely reorganized and came to comprise the following units: four battalions of line infantry, one battalion of light infantry, one regiment of mounted chasseurs, one independent company of cavalry, one battalion of artillery, two battalions of National Guard infantry and one battalion of Militia infantry. The regiment of mounted chasseurs – the "*Cazadores de la Escolta Directorial*" – initially had two squadrons that were later increased to three; it was tasked with acting as the mounted escort of the Chilean government. During 1818–1823 O'Higgins expanded the Chilean Army by creating several new corps: one elite infantry battalion, the "*Guardia de Honor*", in 1818, which was tasked with acting as the foot bodyguard of the Chilean government; one line infantry battalion and one squadron of dragoons in 1819; two line infantry battalions, one regiment of cavalry, one squadron of dragoons (soon disbanded) and one squadron of hussars in 1820; one company of "*carabineros*" (heavy cavalry, soon transformed into a squadron) in 1821; one company (soon transformed into a squadron) of "guides" (light cavalry) in 1822. The latter year saw some organizational changes for the Chilean cavalry, since the hussar squadron formed in 1820 was transformed into a dragoon corps and a new squadron of dragoons, tasked with escort duties, was raised. In 1823 the "*Guardia de Honor*" was expanded and became an elite infantry regiment with two battalions. During that same year a new line infantry battalion became part of the Chilean Army (bringing the total to eight).

After O'Higgins was deposed by a coup of Chilean conservatives during 1823, the Chilean Army entered into a new phase of its history. The "*Guardia de Honor*" went back to its previous establishment with just one battalion of grenadiers, the guard dragoons raised in 1822 assumed the new denomination of "Grenadiers-Lancers" (becoming a regiment) and the squadron of "*carabineros*" was absorbed into the regiment of mounted chasseurs as the latter's fourth squadron. In 1824 the "*Guardia de Honor*" and one of the line infantry battalions were disbanded; in 1825 another line infantry battalion was dissolved; in 1826 the "Grenadiers-Lancers", the light infantry battalion and another line infantry battalion were disbanded. As a result of the progressive de-mobilization described above, the Chilean infantry was reduced from eight line battalions and one light battalion to five line battalions having the following denominations: "*Chacabuco*", "*Carampangue*", "*Maipú*", "*Concepción*" and "*Pudeto*". Each of the latter had one company of grenadiers, one company of *cazadores* and four companies of fusiliers. In July 1827 the cavalry of the Chilean Army was completely reorganized, in order to consist of three consolidated regiments having two squadrons each: the "*Cazadores a Caballo*" (Mounted Chasseurs), formed from the first and second squadron of the mounted chasseur regiment that was already in existence; the "*Granaderos a Caballo*" (Mounted Grenadiers), formed from the third and fourth squadrons of the mounted chasseur regiment that was already in existence; the "*Dragones*" (Dragoons), formed from the existing dragoon corps. In addition to the three new regiments, a new squadron of cuirassiers with two companies was formed. This was tasked with acting as the new mounted bodyguard

Chilean infantryman of the "*Guardia de Honor*" Battalion in 1818. *Colour plate by Patricio Greve Moller, copyright of Gabriele Esposito.*

of the Chilean government. In 1828 the "*Dragones*" Regiment was disbanded and its members were employed to raise a third squadron in both the "*Cazadores a Caballo*" and "*Granaderos a Caballo*". In 1829 the Cuirassier Squadron, which had mutinied, was dissolved and substituted in its guard functions by one squadron (with two companies) of hussars. As regards the infantry, in 1829 the "*Maipú*" Battalion was disbanded and the new "*Valdivia*" Battalion was raised. But in 1830, however, the "*Maipú*" Battalion was re-formed.

The year 1830 saw the outbreak of a brief but significant civil war in Chile, during which the units of the army fought against each other. At the end of the hostilities, three of the line infantry battalions which had supported the side that had been defeated were disbanded. These were "*Chacabuco*", "*Concepción*" and "*Pudeto*". As a result, only three battalions remained: "*Carampangue*", the recently re-formed "*Maipú*" and the newly-raised "*Valdivia*". These were soon supplemented by a new light infantry battalion, named "*Cazadores*". In 1832 the cavalry was expanded with the formation of a new independent company, known as "*Carabineros de la Frontera*", a mounted infantry corps specifically tasked with protecting the southern frontier of Chile from the incursions of the local natives (who were extremely warlike and fought as mounted skirmishers). As regards the artillery, from 1824 it consisted of a foot battalion with three "brigades" and of a mounted squadron with two companies. The first of the foot "brigades" had three companies/batteries, while the other two had two companies/batteries each. As a result, the artillery of the Chilean Army comprised seven foot companies and two mounted companies. In 1827 the horse artillery was reduced to a single company, and by 1830 one of the foot companies had been dissolved. Following the outbreak of the hostilities with the Peru-Bolivian Confederation in 1837, the "*Cazadores*" light infantry battalion was disbanded and the "*Maipú*" Battalion was re-named "*Cazadores de Maipú*". More or less at the same time, the "*Carabineros de la Frontera*" were reorganized as a squadron with two companies. In 1837, the first squadron of the "*Cazadores a Caballo*" was detached from its parent regiment

Chilean infantryman wearing 1823 uniform (left) and trooper of the "*Guides*" Squadron in 1824. *Colour plate by Patricio Greve Moller, copyright of Gabriele Esposito.*

and transformed into an autonomous squadron of lancers. The "*Granaderos a Caballo*" were expanded with the addition of a new squadron equipped with spears, while the "*Cazadores de Maipú*" were transformed into a regiment with two battalions.

During the first military expedition against the Peru-Bolivian Confederation, the Chilean Army was supported by the following corps made up of Peruvian "political exiles" who were loyal to Gamarra: one line infantry battalion, one light infantry battalion and one hussar squadron. These units were all made up of former members of the Peruvian Army. During the second expedition, the Peruvian supporters of Gamarra were re-organized by the Chileans into two infantry battalions: "*Cazadores del Perù*" and "*Huaylas*". During the military preparations for the first expedition against the Peru-Bolivian Confederation, the "*Cazadores de Maipú*" Regiment mutinied against the central government together with two battalions of National Guard infantry that had been recently mobilized. As a result, after the rebellion was crushed the unit was disbanded. Two new line infantry battalions ("*Portales*" and "*Valparaiso*") were thus raised to replace the dissolved corps. During the preparations for the first expedition a new line infantry battalion, the "*Colchagua*", was raised from Chilean volunteers who wanted to fight for their homeland. During the preparations for the second expedition another three line infantry battalions were raised from volunteers: "*Santiago*", "*Aconcagua*" and "*Chillán*". The last of these remained as a garrison in Chile. As a result of the above, the following Chilean infantry battalions participated in the second expedition against the Peru-Bolivian Confederation: "*Carampangue*", "*Valdivia*", "*Portales*", "*Valparaiso*", "*Colchagua*", "*Santiago*" and "*Aconcagua*". During 1838 another three short-lived units were raised: an infantry battalion of volunteers (which remained as garrison in Chile), a company of mounted guides (which operated in Peru conducting scouting missions) and a company of garrison artillery. Following the victorious Battle of Yungay and the dissolution of the Peru-Bolivian Confederation, the Chilean Army was rapidly de-mobilized and many of its newly-formed corps were disbanded.

Chilean cavalryman (left) and artilleryman (right) wearing 1827 uniform. *Colour plate by Patricio Greve Moller, copyright of Gabriele Esposito.*

According to the reorganization of 1840, the Chilean military forces were to comprise the following units: four infantry battalions, the *"Cazadores a Caballo"* Regiment, the *"Granaderos a Caballo"* Regiment, the Hussar Squadron and the Artillery Corps. The four infantry battalions (having six companies each) were named as follows: *"Carampangue"*, *"Valdivia"*, *"Portales"* and *"Yungay"*. The latter absorbed the best elements from the disbanded infantry corps. The lancer squadron of the *"Granaderos a Caballo"* was disbanded, together with the other one that had been formed from the *"Cazadores a Caballo"*. As a result, the two mounted units remained with two squadrons each. The artillery was to be organized as five foot companies and one mounted company. In 1840 a single company of naval infantry was created, which was expanded to become a "brigade" having two companies during 1843. The years following 1840 did not see major modifications for the organization of the Chilean Army, whose quality improved significantly thanks to the creation of the first military academy in 1842. In 1844 the Hussar Squadron, tasked with acting as the mounted bodyguard of the government, was disbanded and substituted with a new squadron of guides. The latter, however, was extremely short-lived since it was disbanded in 1845. The task of providing the presidential mounted escort was thus assigned to the first squadron of the *"Granaderos a Caballo"*. In 1845 the number of line infantry battalions was reduced from four to three (the *"Portales"* Battalion was disbanded) and a new company of foot artillery was raised. The *"Cazadores a Caballo"* were to have three squadrons, the *"Granaderos a Caballo"* were to have two. In 1846 a new line infantry battalion, named *"Chacabuco"*, was created. The military units described above, as previously, were supplemented by a small engineer corps that was made up of a few officers having specific technical skills.

In 1851 a civil war broke out in Chile, the first major one ever experienced by the country. This had significant consequences for the army, which saw some of its units being disbanded and several new corps being raised. The line infantry battalions *"Valdivia"*, *"Yungay"* and *"Chacabuco"* were disbanded because of the indiscipline of their members, while the following new infantry units were formed: five battalions, one garrison company and two depot companies. The cavalry was expanded with the addition of a third squadron to the *"Granaderos a Caballo"* and with the formation of a lancer squadron

Chilean trooper of the *"Cuirassiers"* Squadron in 1828 (left) and trooper of the *"Hussars"* Squadron in 1829 (right). Colour plate by Patricio Greve Moller, copyright of Gabriele Esposito.

("*Lanceros de Colchagua*"). The artillery was augmented by the addition of a new mounted company. In 1852, following the end of the civil war, the Chilean Army was re-structured in the following units: five line infantry battalions with six companies each, "*Granaderos a Caballo*" Regiment, "*Cazadores a Caballo*" Regiment, "*Lanceros de Colchagua*" Squadron and one regiment of artillery (with six foot companies and two mounted companies). In 1854 one of the infantry battalions was disbanded, being followed in 1856 by the single squadron of lancers. During 1857 the "brigade" of naval infantry was expanded and came to have three companies.

In 1859 Chile was shattered by a new civil war and thus the army, as had happened in 1851, was temporarily enlarged with the formation of the following new corps: three infantry battalions, six independent infantry companies, three cavalry squadrons, two independent cavalry companies and one foot artillery company. The rebels who fought against the central government organized their military forces as two line infantry battalions, one company of "*zuavos*" (light infantry) and one squadron of cavalry. In 1860, following the end of the hostilities, the Chilean Army was re-structured in the following corps: five line infantry battalions, "*Granaderos a Caballo*" Regiment, "*Cazadores a Caballo*" Regiment and one artillery regiment (with five foot companies and one mounted company). After Chile entered the Chincha Islands War against Spain, the army was temporarily expanded with the raising of some new corps: four line infantry battalions (one of which, as had happened in 1859, was formed from the gendarmerie of Santiago) and one artillery company. On 4 August 1866, the Chilean marines were reorganized as a Naval Artillery Battalion mustering six companies. After the end of the hostilities, during 1868, the Chilean military forces were reorganized as follows: six line infantry battalions with six companies each, "*Granaderos a Caballo*" Regiment with two squadrons, "*Cazadores a Caballo*" Regiment with three squadrons and one artillery regiment. The latter had five foot companies and one mounted company.

Chilean infantryman (left) and artilleryman (right) wearing 1832 uniform. *Colour plate by Patricio Greve Moller, copyright of Gabriele Esposito.*

Uniforms and weapons

The dress regulations promulgated in 1823, after the coup that removed O'Higgins, prescribed the use of simple but practical uniforms for the Chilean Army. The infantry had to be dressed as follows: dark blue "*bonnet de police*" fatigue cap with red bottom band and unit number on the front, dark blue single-breasted coatee with red collar, red piping to the front and round cuffs, dark blue unit number on the collar and dark blue trousers. The artillery was dressed like the infantry, but with dark blue flaming grenade on the front of the headgear and on the collar. The cavalry was dressed like the infantry, but with dark blue collar piped in red and double red side-stripe on the trousers. Each of the existing cavalry units had a different badge embroidered in red on the collar: a bugle horn for the mounted chasseurs, a flaming grenade for the mounted grenadiers and a saber crossed with a palm branch for the dragoons. The "Guides Squadron" formed in 1824 was dressed as shown in one of the colour pictures. The "*Guardia de Honor*" created by O'Higgins, instead, wore a very ornate uniform with coloured frontal plastron that is shown in one of the colour pictures. From 1826 each of the infantry battalions started to have collars in a distinctive unit colour. In 1827 the cavalry received a new uniform, which was much more "conventional" than the previous one and comprised dark blue single-breasted coatee and dark blue trousers together with a black shako (having the national cockade). The cord of the shako, collar and piping of the coatee were in the distinctive colour of each unit: green for the mounted chasseurs, red for the mounted grenadiers and yellow for the dragoons. The unit badges continued to be embroidered on the collar, in the distinctive colour of each corps. The "Cuirassiers Squadron" was assigned the uniform shown in one of the colour pictures. During 1827 the artillery was also assigned a new uniform with black shako, dark blue single-breasted coatee and dark blue trousers. This had a dark blue collar with yellow flaming grenade and red piping together with red side-stripe on trousers. The shako had a red pompom. The horse artillery was uniformed like the foot one, except for having red frogging on the front of the coatee (which was short-tailed like the cavalry one) and red short plume on the shako instead of the pompom. The "Hussars Squadron" formed in 1829 was dressed as shown in one of the colour pictures. In 1832 the infantry was also assigned the shako as standard headgear and the existing uniforms were slightly modified. Each corps had a distinctive brass badge on the front of the shako: a five-pointed star for the infantry, two crossed cannons for the artillery and the usual badges for the cavalry. The infantry's coatee had red collar and cuff flaps, as well as red piping to the front and round cuffs. The brass initials of each corps' name were applied on the collar. The cavalry's coatee had collar, cuff flaps and piping in green for the mounted chasseurs and in red for the mounted grenadiers; the unit badges were, respectively, a bugle horn and a flaming grenade. The artillery's coatee had collar, cuff flaps and piping in red; the unit badge consisted of a yellow flaming grenade.

On 6 August 1842 new dress regulations were promulgated for the Chilean Army, which introduced the use of the tunic, following the uniform regulations for the French light infantry "*chasseurs*" of 1840 and prescribed the following uniform for the infantry: black shako with national cockade, red top band, brass frontal plate bearing the Chilean coat-of-arms and red pompom; dark blue single-breasted tunic with collar in the distinctive colour of each battalion piped in red, red piping to the front and round cuffs, red cuff flaps; dark blue trousers. The artillery was

Chilean infantryman wearing the service dress prescribed by the 1832 uniform regulations, with "*bonnet de police*" fatigue cap. *ASKB Military Collection*.

dressed like the infantry, but with red collar bearing a yellow flaming grenade. The cavalry had red side-stripe on the trousers and coloured collar: red with dark blue flaming grenade for the "*Granaderos a Caballo*" and green with dark blue bugle horn for the "*Cazadores a Caballo*".

On 29 April 1852 the uniforms described above were abolished due to the promulgation of new dress regulations, which were clearly influenced by the French ones introduced in 1845. The uniform of the infantry became as follows: black shako with national cockade, red top band, brass unit number on the front with two laurel branches and red pompom; dark blue single-breasted tunic with red standing collar and round cuffs; "*garance*" red trousers. The artillery was dressed like the infantry but with a distinctive brass badge on the shako (consisting of two crossed cannons and a flaming grenade), an iron grey frontal plastron on the tunic, pointed cuffs instead of the round ones and dark blue trousers having red side-stripe. The cavalry had black shako with national cockade, top band in regimental colour, brass unit badge on the front and pompom in regimental colour; dark blue tunic with standing collar, pointed cuffs and frontal plastron in regimental colour; "*garance*" red trousers with side-stripe in regimental colour. The "*Cazadores a Caballo*" had green as regimental colour and their badge was a bugle horn; the "*Granaderos a Caballo*" had red as regimental colour and their badge was a flaming grenade. The side-stripe of trousers was dark blue for them. The "*Lanceros de Colchagua*" had yellow as unit colour and their badge consisted of two crossed spears with a five-pointed star. They, in addition, wore a peculiar headgear on parade instead of the shako: black "*czapka*" with brass frontal plate, yellow falling plume, national cockade, red top part and yellow decorative cord. The dress regulations of 1858, which remained valid until 1878, modified only slightly those of 1852; they, in fact, introduced the képi as the new campaign headgear of the Chilean Army. This was red with dark blue bottom band for the infantry, red with green bottom band for the mounted chasseurs, red with dark blue bottom band for the mounted grenadiers and entirely dark blue for the artillery. Since its formation, the naval infantry was dressed quite similarly to the line infantry; in 1866 it received a distinctive uniform consisting of dark blue kepi and dark blue double-breasted tunic having grey facings as well as grey trousers.

As regards weapons, until 1851 the Chilean infantry was equipped with Brown Bess flintlock muskets. From that year significant numbers of new "Minié" M1849 percussion muskets were purchased from France. After the end of the US Civil War, these were supplemented with a certain number of surplus M1861 Springfield muskets acquired in the USA. After the end of the Chincha Islands War, the percussion muskets of the Chilean Army were rapidly replaced with M1867 "Tabatière" breech-loaders produced in France. Until 1852 the Chilean cavalry was mostly equipped with British flintlock carbines and M1796 light cavalry sabres. These were progressively replaced with French "Minié" percussion carbines and M1822 light cavalry sabres.

Chilean infantryman (left) and cavalryman (right) wearing 1842 uniform. *Colour plate by Patricio Greve Moller, copyright of Gabriele Esposito.*

Chilean infantryman (left) and cavalryman (right) wearing 1852 uniform. *Colour plate by Patricio Greve Moller, copyright of Gabriele Esposito.*

The Bolivian Army

History and organization

The Bolivian Army was organized during 1825–1826 by Antonio José de Sucre, one of the most brilliant collaborators of Simón Bolívar and the commander of the Gran Colombian military forces that garrisoned the territory of Bolivia after having expelled the Spaniards from it. Sucre had to face a series of threats while trying to organize Bolivia as an independent republic, since both the Peruvians and the Empire of Brazil were interested in conquering the new state. In 1825, for example, the Brazilians sent a military expedition to occupy the Bolivian frontier province of Chiquitos. For some weeks it seemed that the outbreak of a war between Brazil and Gran Colombia was imminent, but in the end the Brazilians preferred to evacuate the province that they had occupied in order to avoid a direct confrontation with Sucre. The latter, after these events, accelerated the process that led to the formation of an independent Bolivian Army. For the new republic, in fact, it was absolutely necessary to have some well-organized regular troops that could guard its frontiers. Sucre built up the Bolivian Army from the "*Aguerridos*" Battalion, a military unit made up of Bolivian patriots that had fought with distinction against the Spaniards

Left: Bolivian infantryman wearing 1827 uniform. *Colour plate by Patricio Greve Moller, copyright of Gabriele Esposito.*

Right: Bolivian trooper of the "*Lanceros de la Guardia*" wearing 1831 uniform. *Colour plate by Patricio Greve Moller, copyright of Gabriele Esposito.*

during the previous years. Among the members of the "*Aguerridos*" Battalion there were many ambitious young officers, who later became presidents of Bolivia. The unit earned a lot of combat experience by fighting with the use of "guerrilla" tactics. Sucre organized the new Bolivian Army in the following units: two battalions of line infantry, one squadron of lancers and one squadron of artillery. The first of the infantry corps was the former "*Aguerridos*" Battalion.

In 1828, when the Peruvian Army invaded Bolivia, most of the Bolivian Army's units changed sides and abandoned Sucre. The latter tried to defend the Bolivian territory with his Gran Colombian troops, but in the end he was defeated by the Peruvians and had to evacuate the country. After these events, in 1829, the Peruvian general Santa Cruz became the new president of Bolivia, this marking the beginning of a new political phase for the latter country, which was dominated by Peru. Soon after becoming president, Santa Cruz completely reorganized the Bolivian Army. It came to comprise the following units: five battalions of infantry, three regiments of cavalry and one squadron of artillery. During the whole period 1825–1865 the mounted units of the Bolivian Army were frequently designated as regiments, but in most cases they had the numerical make up of a single squadron. Something similar happened for the artillery that, despite its different denominations, always deployed just a very few guns assembled into a single battery. According to the new organization introduced by Santa Cruz, each infantry battalion was to consist of six companies: one of grenadiers, one of *cazadores* and four of fusiliers. The cavalry, at least on paper, was to be structured in regiments having two squadrons with two companies each plus one independent company of "*flanqueadores*" (cavalrymen armed with carbines). In 1831 the 1st Infantry Battalion and the 1st Cavalry Regiment were transformed into guard corps by Santa Cruz. The first became a unit of grenadiers, while the second became a unit of lancers. When Santa Cruz invaded Peru in 1835, the Bolivian Army consisted of the following corps: four infantry battalions, three cavalry regiments and one artillery company. During the mobilization that followed the invasion, the number of infantry battalions was increased to six and a new cavalry regiment was formed. In 1837 another two infantry battalions were raised from members of the National Guard. During 1838 a new cavalry squadron was created in the Bolivian capital of La Paz, in order to garrison the latter. In 1839 the Bolivian military forces were completely annihilated by the

Bolivian grenadier of the guard (left) and cazador of the guard (right) wearing 1842 uniform. *Colour plate by Patricio Greve Moller, copyright of Gabriele Esposito.*

Chileans at the Battle of Yungay, in a clash that led to the fall of Santa Cruz. A period of political anarchy then commenced for Bolivia, which saw several pretenders fighting to obtain the presidency of the state. In this chaotic phase the Bolivian Army was temporarily reorganized in four infantry battalions, two regiments of cavalry (a heavy one and a light one) and one artillery corps.

In 1841 the ambitious and capable José Ballivián emerged as the victor of the civil conflict that had been ravaging Bolivia since 1839. The new president, however, soon had to face the invasion of his country organized by Gamarra. Ballivián had to expand and reorganize the Bolivian military forces in a very short time, but was able to mobilize the following corps for the decisive Battle of Ingavi: two battalions of guard infantry (one of grenadiers and one of *cazadores*), eight battalions of line infantry, two squadrons of guard cavalry (one of mounted grenadiers and one of guides), three squadrons of line cavalry (cuirassiers) and one squadron of artillery (equipped with light pieces). This new army triumphed at Ingavi, mostly thanks to the decisive role played by the line cavalry that Ballivián had recently re-equipped with metal helmets and cuirasses. For this reason, after 1841, most of the cavalry corps included into the Bolivian Army were always equipped as cuirassier ones. In 1842 Ballivián reorganized his military forces and expanded them in a significant way, transforming the Bolivian Army into one of the best combat forces of South America. The presidential guard was re-structured in two battalions of foot grenadiers, one battalion of foot chasseurs and one squadron of mounted grenadiers. The three foot units had six companies each plus one depot company; the mounted grenadiers consisted of a single squadron with two companies. The line infantry was to consist of 12 battalions, each of which had

Bolivian mounted grenadier of the guard (left), cuirassier of the line cavalry (centre) and hussar of the line cavalry (right) wearing 1842 uniform. *Colour plate by Patricio Greve Moller, copyright of Gabriele Esposito.*

four active companies and one depot company of fusiliers. The line cavalry was re-structured in squadrons having two companies each: four squadrons of heavy cavalry cuirassiers and two squadrons of light cavalry hussars. The 2nd Squadron of Hussars was a depot unit, which was to be mobilized in time of war. The artillery was re-structured as a brigade, having two foot companies and two mounted companies (the latter were assembled together to form a squadron). Each artillery company/battery was equipped with four guns, each of the two foot companies comprised a small detachment of sappers. The excellent army forged by Ballivián disappeared after he was forced to leave Bolivia as an exile in December 1847, as the result of an ongoing civil war.

From 1848 the Bolivian Army entered a long period of decline and anarchy, which was characterized by frequent civil conflicts and military coups. The military forces were significantly reduced in their numbers and lost most of their previous discipline. The various dictators emerging during 1848–1865 all gained power thanks to the support they received from the army, whose members strongly influenced Bolivian politics by acting like true "praetorians". The many changes of government very badly affected the Bolivian military units, which were usually reorganised every time a new dictator rose to power. The official denominations of the various corps changed very often, causing great confusion. In addition, after obtaining power, each president usually replaced all the officers of a military unit with individuals who were part of his most loyal supporters. These lacked any form of professionalism and were just interested in pursuing their own political interests. To sum up, from 1848, the phenomenon known as "*caudillismo*" greatly weakened the Bolivian Army. By 1852 the latter had been reorganized in four infantry battalions, two regiments of heavy cavalry (cuirassiers), one squadron of light cavalry (hussars, acting as the mounted bodyguard of the president) and one squadron of artillery. Several of the army's corps were designated as "guard" units. This, however, had a purely honorific function since all the corps had the same uniforms and equipment. In 1855 both regiments of cuirassiers mutinied against the ruling government and thus were disbanded after their members fled to Peru. They were replaced in 1857 by a single squadron of cuirassiers, which was known as "Bolívar". A second squadron of cuirassiers was formed only during 1860. In 1861 the Bolivian Army was reorganized in two infantry battalions, two regiments of cuirassiers, one squadron of hussars and one regiment of artillery. The latter was equipped with just 12 guns. In December 1864 Mariano Melgarejo, an experienced military commander, became the new president of Bolivia. He brought some stability to his nation and ruled until 1871. Melgarejo, after stabilizing his power, re-structured the Bolivian Army in the following corps in September 1867: six infantry battalions, two cavalry squadrons, one regiment of mounted bodyguard and one regiment of artillery. The mounted bodyguard was formed in 1865 and initially consisted of cuirassiers; in 1867 it was transformed into a unit of "*rifleros*" (i.e. light cavalrymen armed with rifled carbines). The regiment was entirely made up of Melgarejo's relatives and supporters.

Bolivian cavalryman wearing 1851 uniform. *Colour plate by Patricio Greve Moller, copyright of Gabriele Esposito.*

Uniforms and weapons

The first official dress regulations for the Bolivian Army were promulgated in January 1827 by Sucre. They prescribed the following uniform for the infantry: black shako with national cockade and brass frontal plate bearing the Bolivian coat-of-arms, dark blue single-breasted coatee with red standing collar and green round cuffs (both having yellow piping), yellow piping to the front of the coatee, yellow badge embroidered on the collar (consisting of a musket crossed with a palm branch) and dark blue trousers. The cavalry was dressed like the infantry, but with green standing collar and red round cuffs; its badge, embroidered on the collar in yellow, consisted of a sabre crossed with a palm branch. The artillery had a coatee with dark blue frontal plastron piped in yellow and black lace on the buttonholes, red collar and cuffs piped in yellow, yellow flaming grenade on the collar and red shoulder straps piped in yellow. The shako and trousers were like those of the infantry. In September 1829 Santa Cruz issued new dress regulations, which prescribed the following uniform for the infantry: black shako with tricolour short plume and pompom, dark blue single-breasted coatee with red standing collar and green round cuffs piped in yellow, red shoulder straps piped in yellow and dark blue trousers. Grenadiers had the short plume of the shako in red, *cazadores* had it in green. The cavalry wore a black bearskin with white decorative cord, red "bag" of cloth on the back, tricolour plume on the left side and metal frontal plate painted in the Bolivian national colours; red single-breasted and short-tailed coatee with yellow standing collar, green pointed cuffs, yellow shoulder straps and yellow piping to the front; dark blue or grey trousers. The "*flanqueadores*" were dressed like the rest of cavalry, but with the same shako as the infantry's *cazadores* as headgear. The artillery was dressed like the infantry, but with red cuffs and with yellow flaming grenade on the collar.

In 1831 Santa Cruz organized two guard units within the Bolivian Army; for the uniform of the cavalry one see the relevant colour picture, while that of the infantry unit was as follows: brown short bearskin made with vicuña wool having yellow decorative cord and plume, brass frontal plate bearing the Bolivian coat-of-arms and the unit's name, red single-breasted coatee with green standing collar and round cuffs piped in yellow, yellow piping to the front of the coatee and dark blue trousers. Grenadiers had a different headgear, consisting of a tall black bearskin having red decorative cord and plume plus green "bag" of cloth on the back. The frontal plate was made of brass, bearing the Bolivian coat-of-arms and the unit's name. The *cazadores* used the shorter version of the bearskin, but with green decorative cord and plume instead of yellow ones. It was with the uniforms described above that the Bolivian Army participated to the military campaigns of the Peru-Bolivian Confederation and repelled the Peruvian invasion of 1841. It should be noted, however, that before the Battle of Ingavi metal helmets and cuirasses were issued to most of the cavalry as ordered by Ballivián.

The latter, as part of his reorganization of the Bolivian military forces, promulgated new dress regulations in 1842. These were extremely colourful and showed a certain French influence. In addition, they introduced uniforms in the three national colours of Bolivia for most of the units (a tradition that was retained for most of the 19th century). For the dress of the foot grenadiers of the guard, *cazadores* of the guard and mounted grenadiers of the guard see the relevant colour pictures. The line infantry was dressed like the foot grenadiers of the guard but without yellow flaming grenade on the collar and with a black shako, having national cockade, brass unit number on the front, red top band and red pompom, as head-

Bolivian infantryman wearing 1856 uniform. *Colour plate by Patricio Greve Moller, copyright of Gabriele Esposito.*

gear. For the uniforms of cuirassiers and hussars see the relevant colour picture. The foot artillery, instead, was dressed as follows: black shako with national cockade, brass flaming grenade on the front, red top band, red decorative cord and red pompom; dark blue long-tailed coatee with red standing collar and round cuffs, dark blue frontal plastron with red piping and red lace on the buttonholes, yellow flaming grenade embroidered on the collar; dark blue trousers with red side-stripe. The coatee of the horse artillery was short-tailed.

The uniforms of the Bolivian Army were changed in 1851, when new dress regulations were promulgated. These prescribed the following uniform for the infantry: black shako with national cockade, brass frontal plate bearing unit number and coloured pompom (yellow for fusiliers, red for grenadiers and green for *cazadores*); dark blue single-breasted coatee with green standing collar and round cuffs; dark blue trousers with light blue side-stripe. The cuirassiers were to be uniformed as shown in one of the colour pictures, while the artillery was dressed similarly to the infantry but with red collar, cuffs and side-stripe of the trousers plus yellow flaming grenade embroidered on the collar. New dress regulations were promulgated in 1856, which introduced a new red uniform for the infantry, with tunic, that is shown in one of the colour pictures. The uniform of the cavalry did not change a lot from that prescribed by the dress regulations of 1851: the dark blue coatee with red facings was replaced by a red tunic with green facings. The artillery's dress was not modified by the new regulations of 1856. The latter were quite short-lived, since in 1858 new uniform regulations were promulgated. These confirmed the use of the tunic and showed a distinct French influence. For the dress of the infantry and of the heavy cavalry, see the relevant colour picture. The light cavalry was uniformed like the cuirassiers, but with a black shako having green falling plume on the front as headgear. The artillery wore the same shako as the infantry (with red short plume), but was dressed as follows: dark green tunic with dark green frontal plastron having red piping, dark green standing collar and pointed cuffs with red piping, dark green shoulder straps with red piping, dark blue trousers with red side-stripe.

With regards to weapons, until the 1850s the Bolivian Army was mostly equipped with British Brown Bess flintlock muskets for the infantry and M1796 light cavalry sabres for the cavalry. These were gradually replaced with British Pattern 1853 Enfield percussion muskets and French M1822 light cavalry sabres.

Bolivian infantryman (left) and cavalryman (right) wearing 1858 uniform. *Colour plate by Patricio Greve Moller, copyright of Gabriele Esposito.*

The Colombian Army

History and organization

The Gran Colombian Army was forged by Simón Bolívar over a long period of time, which began in 1813 when the great patriot leader was able to free a good portion of his country, Venezuela, from Spanish rule. In the following years Bolívar gradually liberated most of present-day Colombia from the Spaniards and thus the revolutionary governments of both Venezuela and Colombia (also known as "*Nueva Granada*") came under his control. In 1819 the great general sponsored the birth of the Gran Colombia Confederation, a new federal republic that was to consist of three autonomous departments: Venezuela, Cundinamarca (Colombia) and Quito (Ecuador). Most of the latter's territory, however, was still under Spanish control and thus the Gran Colombian Army spent most of 1822 fighting in Ecuador against the Spaniards. By the end of 1822 the whole territory of Gran Colombia (including Panama since 1821) had been freed from the remaining Spanish presence and the federal republic had been recognized as an independent nation by the USA. During the following years Gran Colombia became the main driving force of South America's struggle for freedom, playing a prominent role in the liberation of both Peru and Bolivia. The significant military successes of Bolívar, which led to the definitive defeat of the Spaniards in 1825, were made possible by the excellent quality of the Gran Colombian Army. The latter, after 1819, consisted of three main components: the regular units placed under the direct command of Bolívar (which mostly consisted of "guard" corps), the semi-regular units under the orders of the Venezuelan "*caudillo*" Páez and the foreign military corps coming from Great Britain.

Since the beginning of his military campaigns, Bolívar wanted to have a nucleus of loyal soldiers, with regular uniforms and proper training, who could act as his personal guard. He had in mind the model of Napoleon's mighty Imperial Guard, which was part of the French Army but comprised its own sub-units of infantry/cavalry/artillery in order to act as a self-sufficient "miniature army" when needed. The first nucleus of what later be-

Gran Colombian cazador (left), cavalryman (centre) and sapper (right) of Bolívar's Honour Guard wearing 1815 uniform. *Colour plate by Benedetto Esposito, copyright of Gabriele Esposito.*

came the Bolivarian Guard was the so-called "Honour Guard", which was organized in February 1815 by Bolívar. It consisted of one company of grenadiers, one company of *cazadores*, one company of fusiliers, one squadron of cavalry, one artillery detachment and one company of sappers. With the passage of time the Honour Guard started to act as a "model unit" for the whole Gran Colombian Army and not only as the personal guard of Bolívar. The latter gradually transformed several of the best regular units under his command into "guard" corps, in order to count on the loyalty of some battle-hardened veterans and to preserve the stability of his military forces. Until 1818, in fact, the patriot military units were usually quite short-lived. They were often disbanded at the end of a campaign or changed denomination without following a precise rule. In 1818 Bolívar decided to give "guard" status to four of his best infantry battalions: "Rifles", "British Legion", "Barcelona" and "*Bravos de Páez*". The first two, as is clear from their denominations, were mostly made up of British professional soldiers who had joined the patriot army as volunteers; the "Rifles" Battalion was a light infantry corps equipped with rifled carbines, the "British Legion" Battalion was a line infantry corps. The "Barcelona" Battalion was raised from the eastern provinces of Venezuela, where the local insurgents were used to fight against the Spaniards with guerrilla methods. The "*Bravos de Páez*" Battalion, instead, was raised from the western provinces of Venezuela and was made up of Páez's best infantrymen. The "Barcelona" Battalion became known as "*Granaderos de la Guardia*" in November 1819, when it was transformed into an elite heavy infantry corps modelled on Napoleon's Foot Grenadiers of the Imperial Guard. The "*Bravos de Páez*" Battalion, instead, received the new denomination of "*Vencedor*" after having become part of the Bolivarian Guard. During 1819–1821 another four infantry battalions were added to the latter: "*Anzoátegui*" and "*Tiradores*" (made up of Colombians), "*Vargas*" (made up of Venezuelans) and "*Boyacá*" (made up of former Spanish prisoners of war).

In 1821, before the decisive Battle of Carabobo that secured Venezuela's independence forever, Bolívar expanded and reorganized the cavalry of his guard that came to comprise three squadrons, one of dragoons, one of lancers and one of hussars, in addition to the already existing mounted squadron of the Honour Guard. The latter, with the reorganization of 1821, practically ceased to exist. Its foot components were absorbed into the other guard corps, while its mounted squadron became the Bolivarian Guard's new squadron of mounted chasseurs. In addition to the units described above, the Bolivarian Guard comprised (temporarily) another cavalry corps, the so-called "Sacred Squadron". This was entirely made up of supernumerary patriot officers, who were assembled together in order to form an elite light cavalry squadron (which mostly performed escort duties). According to the reorganization of 1821, the Bolivarian Guard was to be organized as a division of the Gran Colombian Army and was to be structured in two brigades. During 1822 the infantry of the guard was expanded with the addition of another three battalions: "*Caracas*" (made

Gran Colombian grenadier of the Bolivarian Guard's "*Granaderos*" Battalion. *Colour plate by Benedetto Esposito, copyright of Gabriele Esposito.*

Gran Colombian rifleman of the Bolivarian Guard's "*Rifles*" Battalion. *Colour plate by Patricio Greve Moller, copyright of Gabriele Esposito.*

up of Venezuelans), "*Bogotá*" (made up of Colombians) and "*Voltígeros*" (made up of former royalist soldiers). The cavalry was also enlarged, with the addition of one squadron of mounted grenadiers and one squadron of mounted guides. All the guard cavalry corps were thus assembled together in order to form a mounted brigade. As a result of the above changes, by 1825 the Bolivarian Guard was the largest component of the Gran Colombian Army and comprised eleven infantry battalions as well as six cavalry squadrons: "Rifles" Battalion, "*Carabobo*" Battalion (former "British Legion"), "*Granaderos*" Battalion, "*Vencedor*" Battalion, "*Valeroso*" Battalion (former "*Anzoátegui*"), "*Tiradores*" Battalion, "*Vargas*" Battalion, "*Boyacá*" Battalion, "*Caracas*" Battalion, "*Bogotá*" Battalion, "*Voltígeros*" Battalion, Dragoon Squadron, Lancer Squadron, Hussar Squadron, Mounted Chasseurs Squadron, Mounted Grenadiers Squadron and Mounted Guides Squadron.

In addition to those that were part of the elite Bolivarian Guard, the Gran Colombian Army also comprised some other regular units. These mostly consisted of infantry, since the patriot cavalry always had a semi-regular nature (it was mostly made up of "*llaneros*", i.e. the gauchos of the Venezuelan plains) while the patriot artillery always remained a small corps usually assembled on an "ad hoc" basis. By 1825 the infantry of the Gran Colombian Army consisted of 25 line battalions and 5 light battalions. Each infantry battalion had one company of grenadiers, one company of *cazadores* and six companies of fusiliers. The cavalry comprised 24 squadrons, of which 18 were of line cavalry and 6 were of light cavalry. The artillery, instead, was organized in 24 independent companies/batteries (several of which performed garrison duties). Since November 1821, the military forces of Gran Colombia also included a single battalion of naval infantry.

The second component of the Gran Colombian Army, i.e. the semi-regular units controlled by Páez, it is important to underline that these never had a proper organization to speak of since they always retained a "militia" character. They mostly consisted of cavalry squadrons made up of "*llaneros*", who were extremely loyal to their leader and who were mobilized only in case of need. The only unit commanded by Páez that had a regular nature was his own "Honour Guard", which was created in 1818 by following the example of Bolívar's Honour Guard. The elite corps consisted of three cavalry squadrons, whose members, all "*llaneros*" who were extremely loyal to their leader, were armed as lancers and uniformed as hussars.

As regards the foreign units of the Gran Colombian Army, it is important to remember that the British government supported Bolívar's military efforts from the beginning of his campaigns. The British provided significant bank loans and massive amounts of weapons to the patriots, since they wanted to see the fall of the Spanish Empire in South America. After the expulsion of the Spaniards, in fact, the commercial monopolies of the colonial period would have ended and South America would have become an immense new market for the British merchants (who were extremely interested in purchasing at low costs the local natural resources). After the end of the Napoleonic Wars in 1815, the British government had to de-mobilize its massive military forces that had recently defeated Napoleon at Waterloo. As a result, many battle-hardened professional soldiers were going to be discarded from the British Army. The Duke of Wellington, trying to find a way to demobilize his army without experiencing problems like mutinies or revolts, had the idea of sending his unemployed veterans to South America where they would fight as "volunteers" in the patriot army of Bolívar. The arrival of thousands of British professional soldiers in Venezuela was extremely important for the patriot cause, since these fighters had great combat experience and were perfectly drilled. They soon made up a fundamental component of Bolívar's troops, playing a prominent role in all the most important battles fought by the Gran Colombian Army. The officers of the British "foreign" units acted as instructors for the locally-raised patriot corps, thus contributing in a decisive way to the general improvement of the latter's quality. As a result of the above, Great Britain gave some fundamental military support to Bolívar's cause but without entering the ongoing conflict in a direct way. The British veterans who went to South America, in fact, engaged on a private basis as volunteers and were paid, at least on paper, by the revolutionary

Gran Colombian fusilier of the Bolivarian Guard's "British Legion" Battalion.
Colour plate by Benedetto Esposito, copyright of Gabriele Esposito.

government. The first British military units went to Venezuela in 1817 and consisted of the following corps: one battalion of riflemen, two squadrons of hussars, two squadrons of lancers and one company of artillery. The "*Rifleros*" Battalion soon became the best unit of Bolívar's foot troops, since it was the only one to be entirely equipped with rifled carbines. It won several battles for the patriot cause and, as we have already seen, became part of the Bolivarian Guard. The two squadrons of hussars were soon assembled together to form a single unit, which fought with distinction until being absorbed into the "Sacred Squadron" already described above. The two squadrons of lancers never became active in South America, because one of them was lost in a storm during the crossing of the Atlantic Ocean; the artillery company existed until 1819.

After the arrival of the first units described above, new expeditions of British volunteers (named after the officers who had organized them) continued to reach South America during 1818–1819. The first of these, known as "MacGregor's Expedition", consisted of the following corps: two line infantry battalions, one light infantry company, one hussar squadron and one artillery company. The second expedition, known as "Elsom's Expedition" and comprising a significant number of soldiers who were veterans of the British Army's Hanoverian units, consisted of one rifle battalion and one hussar squadron. The third expedition, known as "English's Expedition", consisted of one line infantry battalion and one hussar regiment. The new British units arriving in South America during 1818–1819, however, were not of the same quality of those that had left Europe in 1817. Most of them were quite short-lived and participated in just a few significant engagements. An exception to this was represented by the line infantry battalion of "English's Expedition", known as "British Legion" Battalion, which became part, as we have already seen, of the Bolivarian Guard. Following the success of the British volunteers who had gone to South America, new contingents of veterans and adventurers wishing to fight for

Gran Colombian trooper of the Bolivarian Guard's *"Mounted Grenadiers"* Squadron (left) and trooper of the Bolivarian Guard's *"Dragoons"* Squadron (right). *Colour plate by Benedetto Esposito, copyright of Gabriele Esposito.*

Gran Colombia also started to be raised in Ireland. Here an entire "Irish Legion" was formed for service against the Spaniards, which consisted of the following corps: two battalions of rifles, two battalions of light infantry and one regiment of lancers. The Irish Legion lost many of its members due to desertion and tropical diseases soon after crossing the Atlantic. As a result, its corps never reached the planned establishment once in South America and were rapidly disbanded. In October 1819 the surviving elements of the various British corps that had been disbanded were assembled together to form a line infantry unit known as "Albion" Battalion. This fought with distinction in Ecuador before being dissolved in 1823.

In October 1820 the surviving elements of the Irish Legion and of some other recently-dissolved British units were absorbed into the "British Legion" Battalion that assumed the new denomination of "*Cazadores Británicos*". The latter was changed to "*Carabobo*" Battalion in 1821. The unit remained part of the Gran Colombian Army until being disbanded in 1827. By the time of Gran Colombia's dissolution, the only remaining British corps of the Gran Colombian Army was the "Rifles" Battalion, which fought with distinction in the Gran Colombia-Peru War (participating to the Battle of Tarqui) but was completely reorganized with Venezuelan recruits in 1829 and thus lost its original "foreign" character.

The military forces of Nueva Granada

After the end of the hostilities with Peru in 1829, the military forces of Gran Colombia were completely de-mobilized and thus the great army forged by Bolívar disappeared quite rapidly. When the Gran Colombian Confederation was dissolved in 1830, the new state of Nueva Granada (comprising Colombia and Panama) inherited what remained of the former Gran Colombian Army. The years 1830–1832 were characterized by great tension from a political and military point of view, since both Venezuela and Ecuador claimed for themselves some border provinces that belonged – on paper – to Nueva Granada. As a result, the newly-born Colombian Army was quite large during its first years of existence. It consisted of eight line infantry battalions, three squadrons of light cavalry (hussars), one brigade and two independent companies of artillery. At the beginning of 1833, following the end of the frontier tensions with Venezuela and Ecuador, the Colombian Army was partly de-mobilized and came to comprise the following corps: five line infantry battalions, two squadrons and one company of light cavalry, one brigade and two companies of artillery. In 1834 the cavalry was reorganized in three squadrons, while the artillery was re-structured as one battalion and one half-battalion. Each infantry battalion consisted of six companies, i.e. two light companies of "*cazadores*" and four line companies of fusiliers. Each cavalry squadron was

Gran Colombian trooper of the Bolivarian Guard's "*Mounted Chasseurs*" Squadron (left) and trooper of the Bolivarian Guard's "*Hussars*" Squadron. *Colour plate by Benedetto Esposito, copyright of Gabriele Esposito.*

to have two companies, while each artillery battalion was to muster six companies/batteries. The re-structured military forces of Nueva Granada also included a single company of naval infantry, which originated during 1834 from the remnants of Gran Colombia's marine battalion. In 1835 one of the infantry battalions was disbanded and the half-battalion of artillery was replaced with four independent companies tasked with performing garrison duties. In 1838 it was decided to reduce the army to one battalion and five half-battalions of infantry, two squadrons of cavalry and one half-battalion of artillery.

But in 1840, however, the following new structure was adopted: five battalions and three independent companies of infantry, three squadrons of cavalry, one battalion and five independent companies of artillery. In 1841, due to the political instability of Nueva Granada, five infantry battalions and one cavalry squadron were added to the existing corps. The expansion continued in 1842, with the addition of another cavalry squadron and with the reorganization of the artillery into seven independent companies. The various corps were assembled into four divisions, which were also known as "columns". In 1844 the Colombian Army was re-structured again. The infantry was to have eight battalions, the cavalry three squadrons and the artillery ten companies/batteries. The infantry battalions were to have six companies each, but in practice they mustered from a minimum of three to a maximum of six companies. The ten artillery companies were assembled into larger units as follows: one battalion with four companies in Cartagena, one half-battalion with two companies in Cundinamarca, one half-battalion with two companies in the southern provinces of Nueva Granada, one independent company in Santa Marta and one independent company in Panama. In 1844 the infantry was reduced to six battalions and one half-battalion (the latter was garrisoned in Panama), the cavalry was consolidated as a single regiment with three squadrons and the artillery was re-structured in two half-battalions and three independent companies (one of which garrisoned Panama). In 1845 the single company of naval infantry was disbanded. In 1846 the half-battalion of the infantry was dissolved and the artillery was re-structured in one battalion, one half-battalion and one independent company. In addition, one half-battalion and three companies of sappers were raised. After these changes, the number of infantry battalions was soon increased to nine and the artillery battalion was transformed into a half-battalion. The new units of sappers were made up of former infantrymen and artillerymen, tasked with constructing public infrastructure in time of peace. In 1848 the Colombian Army had six infantry battalions, one regiment of cavalry, two half-battalions and one company of artillery, one half-battalion and one company of sappers.

In 1849 the government of Nueva Granada, hoping to stop the outbreak of military rebellions that were extremely frequent in Colombia, decided to reduce the army in a drastic way. The military forces were thus reorganized into three small "columns" that comprised the following corps: one battalion and five half-battalions of infantry, one squadron of cavalry, two half-battalions and one company of artillery. It was with

Left: Gran Colombian trooper of the *"Sacred Squadron"*. *Colour plate by Benedetto Esposito, copyright of Gabriele Esposito.*

Right: Gran Colombian trooper of Páez's Honour Guard wearing 1818 uniform. *Colour plate by Benedetto Esposito, copyright of Gabriele Esposito.*

these scarce military forces that the central government entered the civil war of 1851. After the end of the latter, the Colombian Army was re-structured as follows: five battalions and two half-battalions of infantry, one regiment of cavalry with two squadrons, three battalions (with four companies each) and two independent companies of artillery. During 1854–1862 Nueva Granada was shattered by two bloody civil wars, which practically destroyed the regular military forces. Anarchy dominated for several years, until a new federalist constitution was promulgated in 1863. According to this, the territory of Nueva Granada was reorganized as nine autonomous "states", each to have its own independent military forces and thus the regular central army was disbanded. In any case, in order to have some military corps placed under the orders of the central government, a para-military force of gendarmerie known as "*Guardia Colombiana*" was raised to replace the regular army in most of its functions. At the time of its disbandment, the Colombian Army was quite large since it had been expanded due to the civil war and the border war with Ecuador. As a result, it consisted of the following corps: nine infantry battalions, one cavalry regiment, one half-battalion of artillery and one battalion of sappers. These units were all made up of skilled veterans, who were mostly absorbed into the newly-raised "*Guardia Colombiana*". The latter came to comprise the following corps: five infantry battalions, one cavalry regiment, two artillery battalions and one sapper battalion. The infantry was structured in two divisions, while the other units formed a "mixed legion". Each of the new autonomous "regional states" that made up Colombia was to provide a number of recruits for the formation of the "*Guardia Colombiana*", according to quotas that were fixed every year by the central government. The regional governments, however, never collaborated in a positive way with the central authorities since they preferred having stronger regional armies and a weaker "*Guardia Colombiana*". As a result, by 1866, the latter had been significantly reduced and deployed the following corps: two infantry battalions with four companies each, one infantry half-battalion with two companies, one squadron of cavalry (mounted guides), one artillery battalion with four companies/batteries and one sapper battalion with four companies. All these units were structured as a single division. By 1871 the infantry had been reorganized in three battalions and one independent company, while the cavalry had been dissolved. The various corps were scattered over the Colombian territory in small detachments and thus the whole "*Guardia Colombiana*" was much weaker than the military contingents deployed by the regional governments. It continued to exist until 1885, when the regular Colombian Army was finally re-formed. As regards the military forces of the various regional governments, it is important to underline that they had a distinct "militia" character; they were semi-regular at best, lacking proper discipline and uniforms. All the able-bodied male individuals aged 18–60 were to serve in the military contingents of their home territory, but in time of peace only a small number of them was selected for active service. The various regional contingents were political instruments in the hands of the local "*Caudillos*" who ruled the nine autonomous states that made up Colombia; as a result, they frequently fought against each other.

Uniforms and weapons

The first dress regulations for the regular military forces commanded by Bolívar were promulgated on 1 November 1813. These prescribed the following uniform for all the branches of service: black shako with national cockade and coloured pompom, dark blue single-breasted coatee with red standing collar and round cuffs, red piping to the front of the coatee and dark blue trousers. The light infantry, line cavalry and light cavalry had a single-breasted jacket without tails instead of the coatee; the line cavalry, in addition, had white frogging on the front of the jacket. The artillery had the coatee but with yellow flaming grenades embroidered on the collar. The pompom of the infantry's shako was red for grenadiers, green for *cazadores* and yellow for fusiliers; the cavalry shako had a red plume, while the artillery one had a red pompom. The "British Legion" Battalion and the "Albion" Battalion were dressed like the rest of the line infantry, but their coatees were red with light blue facings in order to show the British origins of their members (see the relevant colour picture). The "Rifles" Battalion was uniformed in dark green with black facings, exactly like the rifle corps of the contemporary British Army (see one of the colour pictures).

Gran Colombian NCO of the light infantry wearing 1826 uniform. *Plate and copyright of Eduardo Espinosa Mora.*

Gran Colombian trooper of the line cavalry (left) and trooper of the light cavalry (right) wearing 1826 uniform. *Colour plate by Patricio Greve Moller, copyright of Gabriele Esposito.*

The unit of British hussars absorbed into the "Sacred Squadron" was uniformed in red very similarly to the latter; see one of the colour pictures for the dress of the "Sacred Squadron".

In July 1826 new dress regulations were promulgated for the Gran Colombian Army, which continued to be followed for some time after the dissolution of Gran Colombia by the armies of the three new states that were formed in 1830 (Colombia, Venezuela and Ecuador). For the 1826 uniforms of the line infantry, light infantry, line cavalry, light cavalry and foot artillery see the relevant colour pictures. The line infantry had dark blue single-breasted coatee with red facings, the light infantry had dark blue single-breasted jacket with light blue facings, the line cavalry had dark blue coatee with frontal plastron and yellow facings, the light cavalry had dark blue jacket with frontal plastron and green facings, the foot artillery had dark blue coatee with frontal plastron and red facings, the horse artillery had dark blue jacket with frontal plastron and red facings. The sappers, who were attached to the artillery, were dressed with a grey single-breasted jacket having red facings. The battalion of naval infantry was dressed very similarly to the line infantry. For the uniforms of Bolívar's Honour Guard, see the relevant pictures. The grenadiers, *cazadores* and fusiliers all had the same dress with bearskin and the sappers were uniformed similarly. The cavalry's dress was modelled on that of Napoleon's Mounted Chasseurs of the Imperial Guard. The infantry battalions of the Bolivarian Guard were always dressed like the line infantry of the Gran Colombian Army, thus following the dress regulations of 1813 and of 1826. Only the "*Granaderos*" Battalion had a much more ornate uniform, which is shown in one of the colour pictures. This had a massive black bearskin as headgear only for the grenadier company, since the company of *cazadores* and the companies of fusiliers wore ordinary shakos. The "*Anzoátegui*" Battalion was the only one to have a grey coatee instead of the usual dark blue one. For the ornate uniforms of the six cavalry squadrons included into the Bolivarian Guard as well as for the hussar dress of Páez's Honour Guard, see the relevant colour pictures.

The infantry of the Gran Colombian Army was armed with Brown Bess muskets, while the cavalry carried British M1796 light cavalry sabres.

Until the promulgation of its first dress regulations in 1834, the Colombian Army continued to wear the uniforms prescribed by the 1826 dress regulations of Gran Colombia. In any case, the uniforms introduced in 1834 were almost identical to those that were already in use; for more details about them, see the relevant colour picture. The infantry

---

Colombian infantryman (left), cavalryman (centre) and artilleryman (right) wearing 1834 uniform. *Colour plate by Patricio Greve Moller, copyright of Gabriele Esposito.*

had black shako with national cockade, yellow pompom and cord, brass oval plate bearing unit number; dark blue single-breasted coatee with red standing collar, round cuffs and shoulder straps; yellow piping; dark blue trousers with yellow side-stripe. The cavalry had black shako with national cockade, green pompom and cord, brass oval plate bearing unit number; dark blue single-breasted coatee with green standing collar, round cuffs and piping; dark blue trousers with green side-stripe. The artillery had black shako with national cockade, red pompom and cord, brass badge bearing flaming grenade; dark blue coatee with dark blue standing collar and round cuffs piped in red, dark blue frontal plastron piped in red; dark blue trousers with red side-stripe. The naval infantry was uniformed similarly to the line infantry. New dress regulations were promulgated in 1849, extremely innovative by the standards of contemporary South America, since they introduced the use of the tunic and followed the 1845 dress regulations of the French Army. The infantry, as shown in the relevant colour picture, wore a dark blue tunic with red standing collar and round cuffs piped in dark blue; the cuff flaps were red with dark blue piping, the shoulder straps were dark blue with red piping and the front of the tunic was piped in red. The trousers were entirely "*garance*" red; the black shako had national cockade, brass frontal plate bearing the coat-of-arms of Nueva Granada, red top band and red pompom. The few sappers attached to each infantry battalion were to wear a brown bearskin and carried a massive axe together with a white leather apron and white leather gauntlet-shaped gloves. The cavalry, as shown in the relevant colour picture, was assigned a very ornate hussar-style dress with dark blue dolman and pelisse. The artillery was uniformed like the infantry, but with a different brass plate on the front of the shako (bearing two crossed cannons). The dress regulations of 1849 remained valid until the abolition of the regular army. The irregulars who fought in the civil wars of the 1850s and the militiamen of the regional contingents that became autonomous in 1863 were mostly dressed with irregular civilian clothes; for more details, see the two relevant colour pictures. No official uniform regulations were promulgated for the "*Guardia Colombiana*"; the latter's members, however, were mostly dressed with dark blue short jacket and white trousers. The headgear could be a dark blue képi or a black shako.

During the 1850s the weapons dating back to the period of Gran Colombia were partly substituted with British Pattern 1853 Enfield muskets and French M1822 light cavalry sabres.

Colombian infantryman (left) and cavalryman (right) wearing 1849 uniform. *Colour plate by Patricio Greve Moller, copyright of Gabriele Esposito.*

Colombian officer of the *"Guardia Colombiana"*.

Colombian infantryman of the *"Guardia Colombiana"*.

The Venezuelan Army

History and organization

The Venezuelan Army was organized as an independent military entity during 1830, soon after the splitting of Gran Colombia. Initially it consisted of the following units: two battalions and four independent companies of infantry, two squadrons and one independent company of cavalry, seven companies of artillery. During the second half of 1830 these were supplemented by the "*Boyacá*" Battalion of the former Bolivarian Guard, which was on garrison duty in Colombia but decided to enter Venezuelan service since most of its members were now Venezuelans. Before the end of 1830 the Venezuelan Army was re-structured in the following corps: three battalions and two independent companies of infantry, one squadron of cavalry and six companies of artillery. Two of the infantry battalions – the "*Anzoátegui*" and the "*Boyacá*" – had previously been part of the Bolivarian Guard, exactly like the cavalry squadron (which was the former Mounted Grenadiers Squadron of the Bolivarian Guard). Each of the infantry battalions had one company of grenadiers, one company of *cazadores* and four companies of fusiliers; the single cavalry squadron had two companies. During the last months of 1830, while

Left: Venezuelan infantryman wearing 1836 uniform. *Colour plate by Giuseppe Rava, copyright of Gabriele Esposito.*

Right: Venezuelan artilleryman wearing 1836 uniform. *Colour plate by Patricio Greve Moller, copyright of Gabriele Esposito.*

political tension was extremely high between Venezuela and Nueva Granada, the "Rifles" Battalion of the former Bolivarian Guard, which was in garrison in Colombia, crossed the border to enter Venezuelan service since most of its members were Venezuelans. The president of Venezuela, José Antonio Páez, however, had doubts about the loyalty of the battalion and feared that it could revolt against him. As a result, he decided to disband the glorious "Rifles" Battalion that had fought so well for the independence of South America. Páez never expanded the Venezuelan Army during his long period of rule, preferring to have a small regular force instead of a larger one. He feared that the army could rebel against his government and thus always sponsored the establishment of a strong semi-regular "National Militia" that could be mobilized in case of need. The Militia was mostly recruited from the "*llaneros*" who were extremely loyal to Páez and thus was an instrument in the hands of the latter.

By 1835 the Venezuelan Army had been slightly reduced in its numbers and comprised the following units: three battalions and one independent company of infantry, one company of cavalry and six companies of artillery. In 1836 one infantry battalion, the company of cavalry and three companies of artillery were disbanded. The remaining artillery companies were assembled together into a half-brigade. Each of the remaining infantry battalions was to have just four companies. In 1838 two companies of *cazadores* were added to each infantry battalion and three new half-battalions of infantry were formed to perform garrison duties. In 1841 the regular forces were re-structured as follows: one line infantry battalion with four companies, four independent companies of garrison infantry (soon reduced to two), one squadron of cavalry and one company of artillery. In 1846 the army was significantly enlarged to face the peasant revolts inspired by the liberals who opposed Páez. As a result, it came to comprise the following units: three infantry battalions with six companies each, one cavalry regiment with two squadrons, one artillery brigade with three companies and one sapper corps with three companies. After the civil war of 1848–1849 and the removal of Páez, the Venezuelan Army was re-structured as follows: two infantry battalions with six companies each, two half-brigades of artillery with two companies each and one cavalry squadron with two companies. In 1854 the Venezuelan Army was expanded in a significant way and came to have the following corps: four battalions and one independent company of infantry, one squadron of cavalry and two brigades of artillery with four companies each. In 1858, however, the Venezuelan regular forces were again reduced in their numbers and thus came to comprise the following units: three battalions and two independent companies of infantry, one squadron of

Left: Venezuelan infantryman of the Federal War, wearing 1826 service dress. *Colour plate by Giuseppe Rava, copyright of Gabriele Esposito.*

Right: Venezuelan trooper of the National Militia's cavalry during the Federal War, wearing 1830 uniform. *Colour plate by Patricio Greve Moller, copyright of Gabriele Esposito.*

cavalry, one battalion of artillery and one battalion of sappers. The infantry battalions were named "*Araure*", "*Caracas*" and "*Maturín*"; the cavalry squadron was a corps of mounted guides, while the artillery battalion had four companies. It was with this organization that the Venezuelan Army entered the bloody "Federal War" in 1859.

The liberal insurgents who fought against the central government organized their military forces in four infantry battalions: "*Federación*", "*Flanqueadores*", "*Vanguardia*" and "*Veinte de Febrero*". By 1860 the regular army had been almost destroyed in combat and could deploy just one infantry battalion together with one squadron of cavalry and one half-battalion of artillery. A second infantry battalion was formed in the last months of 1860 by assembling together the best elements of the "*Milicia Nacional*" who had remained loyal to the central government. In 1865, following the end of the Federal War, the Venezuelan Army was temporarily re-structured in four "divisions" (battalions) of infantry and two "brigades" (half-battalions) of artillery. During 1873–1874 the Venezuelan military forces were completely reorganized by the new president, Antonio Guzmán Blanco, and came to muster the following units: one infantry regiment with two battalions, one infantry battalion, three half-battalions of infantry, four infantry "columns" with four companies each, six independent companies of infantry, one artillery brigade with four companies and one half-brigade of artillery with two companies. The single infantry regiment had guard status and was garrisoned in the Venezuelan capital of Caracas. It consisted of liberal veterans who had fought in the Federal War and who were extremely loyal to Guzmán Blanco.

Venezuelan infantryman (left), cavalryman (centre) and artilleryman (right) wearing 1873 uniform. *Colour plate by Patricio Greve Moller, copyright of Gabriele Esposito.*

Uniforms and weapons

Until the promulgation of its first dress regulations in 1836, the Venezuelan Army continued to wear the uniforms prescribed by the 1826 dress regulations of Gran Colombia. In any case, the uniforms introduced in 1836 were almost identical to those that were already in use. The infantry had black shako with national cockade, yellow pompom and cord, brass oval plate bearing unit number; dark blue single-breasted coatee with red standing collar and round cuffs; yellow piping; dark blue trousers with red side-stripe. The cavalry had black shako with national cockade, green pompom and cord, brass oval plate bearing unit number; dark blue single-breasted coatee with green standing collar, round cuffs and piping; dark blue trousers with green side-stripe. The artillery had black shako with national cockade, red pompom and cord, brass badge bearing flaming grenade; dark blue coatee with dark blue standing collar and round cuffs piped in red, dark blue frontal plastron piped in red, yellow flaming grenade embroidered on the collar; dark blue trousers with red side-stripe. The great political instability experienced by Venezuela from 1846 prevented the promulgation of new dress regulations and thus the uniforms introduced in 1836 remained unchanged, at least on paper, during the whole period covered in the present book. It should be noted, however, that from the early 1850s the regular army started to replace its dark blue uniforms with the service dress prescribed by the 1826 regulations of Gran Colombia. This, as shown in the relevant colour picture, com-

Venezuelan/Colombian irregular infantryman from the civil wars of the period 1845–1865. *Colour plate by Patricio Greve Moller, copyright of Gabriele Esposito.*

Venezuelan/Colombian irregular cavalryman from the civil wars of the period 1845–1865. *Colour plate by Patricio Greve Moller, copyright of Gabriele Esposito.*

prised a red "*bonnet de police*" fatigue cap with dark blue bottom band and red tassel that was worn together with white short jacket having red facings and white trousers. It was with this campaign dress that the Venezuelan Army fought in the Federal War. Officers were uniformed differently from their men, with non-regulation dark blue képis and tunics. Most of the Venezuelan military corps that fought in the Federal War were militia ones, which were dressed with the simple uniform introduced for the "*Milicia Nacional*" in 1830. This, as shown in one of the colour pictures, consisted of a round straw hat with national cockade that was worn together with white short jacket and white trousers. The facings of the jacket were red for the infantry, green for the cavalry and blue for the artillery. The officers of the National Militia had dark blue short jackets instead of the white ones worn by their men. The liberal insurgents who fought against the central government in the war of 1859–1863 had no uniforms to speak of and were dressed in their civilian clothes (see the two relevant colour pictures).

In 1873 Guzmán Blanco, who reorganized the Venezuelan Army after 15 years of anarchy, promulgated new dress regulations. These prescribed a new standard uniform consisting of black shako, dark blue short tunic and dark blue trousers (see the relevant colour picture). The infantry shako had yellow pompom and cord, the cavalry shako had yellow short plume and white cord, the artillery shako had red pompom and yellow cord. The standing collar and round cuffs of the tunic were red for the infantry, yellow for the cavalry and dark blue with red piping for the artillery. The latter's tunic had dark blue frontal plastron piped in red and yellow flaming grenade on the collar. The few sappers attached to each infantry battalion were dressed like the infantrymen, but in grey with red facings. With service/campaign dress the shako was replaced by a dark blue képi.

As regards weapons, until 1860 the Venezuelan Army was mostly equipped with old-fashioned Brown Bess flintlock muskets. During the Federal War, however, significant numbers of percussion weapons (M1842 Springfield muskets and Pattern 1853 Enfield muskets) were purchased in the USA. Guzmán Blanco completely re-equipped the Venezuelan infantry with M1867 Remington "Rolling Block" rifles during the early 1870s.

The Ecuadorian Army

History and organization

The Ecuadorian Army was organized as an independent military entity during 1830, soon after the splitting of Gran Colombia. Initially it consisted of just three battalions of infantry and two squadrons of cavalry, which had been part of the Gran Colombian Army. The infantry units were named "*Cauca*", "*Vargas*" and "*Girardot*"; the cavalry corps were known as "*Cedeño*" and "*Yaguachi*". Most of the new Ecuadorian Army's units were made up of Venezuelans, who wanted to leave Ecuador now that Gran Colombia had dissolved. Also the first president of Ecuador, Juan José Flores, was a Venezuelan. The first years of life of the Ecuadorian Army were quite turbulent: in 1831, for example, the "*Vargas*" Battalion rebelled against the central government and was disbanded. Following these events, the cavalry was re-structured in two "regiments" (which continued to have the numerical consistency of squadrons) and the first permanent artillery corps (consisting of a single company) was established. The two remaining infantry battalions had six companies each, while the cavalry units had two companies each. In 1832 the "*Girardot*" Battalion also rebelled against the central government, causing serious problems to the latter.

In 1834 a large scale civil war broke out in Ecuador, which saw the establishment of two rival governments, one supported by Flores in Guayaquil and one guided by José Félix Valdivieso in Quito. During most of the 19th century the two major cities of Ecuador, Quito in the north and Guayaquil in the south, had contrasting interests. The first was dominated by the Ecuadorian conservatives, while the latter was dominated by the Ecuadorian liberals. For these reasons, most of the Ecuadorian civil conflicts were usually fought between rival governments that were established in these two cities. Following the outbreak of the civil war, the Ecuadorian Army entered a state of anarchy. Flores, who could count on the support of the many Venezuelans who were part of the Ecuadorian Army, organized his military forces as one strong infantry battalion ("*Volteadores*") and one cavalry regiment. His opponents deployed four weak infantry battalions and three cavalry squadrons but could also count on some artillery pieces. In 1835, at the Battle of Miñarica, Flores obtained a decisive victory and thus brought back the whole of Ecuador under his control. After the end of the hostilities, during 1835–1836, the Ecuadorian Army was completely reorganized. All the foreign components of the various units were encouraged to leave Ecuador and were replaced with Ecuadorian recruits; a new conscription law, in fact, was promulgated. The Ecuadorian military forces assumed the general structure that they retained for

Ecuadorian infantryman (left) and cavalryman (right) wearing 1833 uniform. *Colour plate by Patricio Greve Moller, copyright of Gabriele Esposito.*

most of the 19th century. They came to consist of two infantry battalions, two regiments (squadrons) of cavalry and one company of artillery. The 2nd Cavalry Squadron was tasked with acting as the mounted bodyguard of the government. During 1838–1842 the infantry was temporarily expanded with the addition of a third battalion. In 1845 Flores left Ecuador as an exile after having been deposed. The Ecuadorian Army that he left behind had seen no major modifications during the previous years, except for the reorganization of the artillery as a half-brigade with two companies. During the civil war of 1845, which led to the removal of Flores, the liberals of Guayaquil revolted against the central government and organized their own military forces that consisted of the following corps: two light infantry battalions ("*Libertador*" and "*Guayas*") with six companies each, three squadrons of lancers and one half-brigade of artillery with two companies.

In 1851 the presidency of Ecuador was assumed by José María Urbina, who decided to promulgate a series of new laws in order to improve the general quality of the Ecuadorian Army. The infantry continued to consist of two battalions having six companies each, which were supplemented by some small detachments tasked with performing garrison duties. The cavalry continued to have two squadrons of lancers with two companies each, but a new cavalry squadron specifically tasked with acting as the mounted bodyguard of Urbina was also formed. This new corps was known as "*Taura*" Squadron and its members were known as "*Tauras*" because it was made up of black soldiers (former slaves) coming from the wild countryside of Taura in southern Ecuador. The "*Tauras*" soon became the "praetorians" of Urbina, suppressing any internal revolt by employing very harsh methods. As regards the artillery, in 1851 it was expanded to become a brigade with four companies/batteries. Following the fall of Urbina in 1856, Ecuador entered a new period of anarchy, with two rival governments established (one in Quito and one in Guayaquil) while the Peruvians invaded southern Ecuador during 1858. As a result of the Peruvian attack, one of the existing foot artillery companies was transformed into a mounted one. In 1861, after Ecuador was re-unified, the regular military units were re-structured in the following corps: three battalions of infantry with six companies each, two regiments of cavalry with four squadrons each and one brigade of artillery with four companies.

Ecuadorian infantry drummer (left) and cavalry trooper (right) of the insurgent forces that fought against Flores in the civil war of 1834–1835. *Plate and copyright of Eduardo Espinosa Mora.*

Uniforms and weapons

Until the promulgation of its first dress regulations in 1833, the Ecuadorian Army continued to wear the uniforms prescribed by the 1826 dress regulations of Gran Colombia. In any case, the uniforms introduced in 1833 were almost identical to those that were already in use (as shown in the relevant colour picture). The infantry had black shako with national cockade, green pompom and cord; dark blue single-breasted coatee with light blue facings; dark blue trousers. The cavalry had black shako with national cockade, red short plume and white cord; dark blue single-breasted coatee with red facings; dark blue trousers. The artillery had black shako with national cockade, red pompom and cord; dark blue single-breasted coatee with red facings and yellow flaming grenade on collar; dark blue trousers. The rebel forces who fought against Flores in the civil war of 1834–1835 wore peculiar uniforms, which are reproduced in one of the colour pictures. The infantry had yellow "*bonnet de police*" with green bottom band and tassel as well as red single-breasted coatee with light blue facings; the cavalry had white "*bonnet de police*" with red bottom band and tassel as well as green dolman with white frogging and violet trousers.

In 1844, shortly before Flores left Ecuador, new dress regulations were promulgated. These prescribed the following uniform for the infantry: black shako with national cockade, dark blue coatee with red frontal plastron and facings, yellow piping to collar, yellow unit badge embroidered on the collar (consisting of a musket crossed with a sabre) and dark blue trousers. The cavalry had black shako with national cockade, red coatee with light blue frontal plastron and facings, red piping to collar, red unit badge embroidered on the collar (consisting of a spear crossed with a sabre) and dark blue trousers. The artillery had black shako with national cockade, dark blue coatee with red frontal plastron and facings, yellow piping to collar, yellow unit badge embroidered on the collar (consisting of two crossed cannons) and dark blue trousers. The military forces organized by the liberal government of Guayaquil during the civil war of 1845 wore regular uniforms; for more details about them, see the relevant colour picture. The infantry was dressed in dark blue with green facings, while the cavalry was dressed in red with light blue facings. The artillery was uniformed exactly as prescribed by the 1844 dress regulations. After the end of the civil war, in

Ecuadorian infantryman (left) and cavalryman (right) wearing 1844 uniform.
Colour plate by Patricio Greve Moller, copyright of Gabriele Esposito.

1846, new uniform regulations were promulgated for the Ecuadorian Army. These prescribed the following dress for the infantry: black shako with national cockade, green cord and brass frontal plate bearing unit number; dark blue single-breasted coatee with green facings and white trousers with green side-stripe. The cavalry had black shako with national cockade, white cord and white metal frontal plate bearing unit number; red single-breasted and short-tailed coatee with light blue facings and dark blue trousers with white side-stripe. The artillery had black shako with national cockade and red cord, dark blue single-breasted and short-tailed coatee with red facings and dark blue trousers with red side-stripe.

In 1863, following the chaotic civil wars and Peruvian invasion of 1856–1860, new dress regulations were promulgated by president Gabriel García Moreno (who re-unified Ecuador and re-organized the military forces). The new uniform regulations were clearly inspired to those of the contemporary French Army and introduced the use of the tunic; for more details about them, see the two relevant colour pictures. The infantry wore dark blue shako with national cockade, pompom in the national colours of Ecuador and brass frontal plate bearing the Ecuadorian coat-of-arms; dark blue tunic with red standing collar, round cuffs and frontal piping; "*garance*" red trousers with dark blue side-stripe. The few sappers attached to each infantry battalion wore a massive bearskin having red cord and coloured plume; they also had red epaulettes on the shoulders, red unit badge embroidered on the left sleeve (consisting of two crossed axes), white leather apron and white leather gauntlet-shaped gloves. The cavalry had black shako with national cockade and white falling plume, dark blue tunic with red standing collar and pointed cuffs, red piping to the front of the tunic, white "contre-epaulettes" and dark blue trousers with red side-stripe. The artillery wore dark blue shako with national cockade, red cord, red short plume and brass frontal plate bearing the Ecuadorian coat-of-arms; dark blue tunic with red standing collar, round cuffs, frontal plastron and epaulettes; dark blue trousers with red double side-stripe.

Until the last years of the 1850s, the Ecuadorian Army was mostly equipped with old-fashioned Brown Bess flintlock muskets and British M1796 light cavalry sabres. During the years 1856–1860, however, a significant number of Pattern 1853 Enfield muskets was purchased together with French M1822 light cavalry sabres.

Ecuadorian infantryman (left) and cavalryman (right) of the insurgent forces that fought against Flores in the civil war of 1845. *Colour plate by Patricio Greve Moller, copyright of Gabriele Esposito.*

Ecuadorian infantryman (left) and cavalryman (right) wearing 1846 uniform. *Colour plate by Patricio Greve Moller, copyright of Gabriele Esposito.*

Ecuadorian infantryman (left) and cavalryman (right) wearing 1863 uniform. *Colour plate by Patricio Greve Moller, copyright of Gabriele Esposito.*

Ecuadorian infantry sapper wearing 1863 uniform. *Plate and copyright of Eduardo Espinosa Mora.*

Select Bibliography

Ayala Mora, E., *Ecuador del Siglo XIX. Estado Nacional, Ejército, Iglesia y Municipio*, Universidad Andina Simón Bolívar, 2011
Barroso, G., *Historia Militar do Brasil*, Rio de Janeiro, 1938
Caronte, L. C., *Legiones Italianas*, Buenos Aires, 1907
Chacon Izurieta, G. E., *Batalla de Miñarica*, Quito, 1985
Diaz Arguedas, J., *Historia del Ejército de Bolivia 1825–1932*, La Paz, 1940
Ejército Uruguayo, *Historia del Ejército*, Montevideo, 2008
Esposito, G., *Storia politico-diplomatico-militare del Venezuela, 1830–1903*, LEG Edizioni, 2022
Estado Mayor General del Ejército de Chile, *Historia del Ejército de Chile*, Santiago de Chile, 1981–1985
Estado Mayor General del Ejército de Colombia, *Historia de las Fuerzas Militares de Colombia*, Bogotá, 1993
Estado Mayor General del Ejército de Ecuador, *Historia General del Ejército Ecuatoriano*, Quito, 2007–2010
Estado Mayor General del Ejército del Perù, *Compendio de la Historia General del Ejército del Perù*, Lima, 2001
Estado Mayor General del Ejército del Perù, *Evolución histórica de los uniformes del Ejército del Perù (1821–1980)*, Lima, 2005
Fernandez Asturizaga, A., *Uniformes Militares Bolivianos 1825–1988*, La Paz, 1991
Ferrer Llul, F., *Sinopsis Gráfica de la Historia Militar del Uruguay*, Montevideo, 1975
Fletcher, J., *Adventures of the British and Irish Legions in South America 1817–1824*, Grenadier Productions, 2011
Hooker, T. D., *Armies of the 19th Century: The Americas – The Paraguayan War*, Foundry Books, 2008
Luqui-Lagleyze, J. M., *Los Cuerpos Militares en la Historia Argentina. Organización y Uniformes 1550–1950*, Instituto Nacional Sanmartiniano, 1995
Lynch, J., *The River Plate Republics from Independence to the Paraguayan War*, in "The Cambridge History of Latin America", Vol. 3, University of Cambridge, 1985
Marquez Allison, Al., Marquez Allison An., *Cuatro Siglos de Uniformes en Chile*, Santiago de Chile, 1975
Martinez Garnica, A., *Historia de la Guardia Colombiana*, Bucaramanga, 2012
Memorial del Ejército de Chile, *Historia de la formación y desarollo del Ejército de Chile de 1541 a 1910*, Santiago de Chile, 1960
Mugnai, B., *Garibaldi in Sudamerica. Gli anni dell'esilio e della lotta 1835–1848*, Soldiershop Publishing, 2014
Olmedo Alvarenga, A., *Historia Militar del Paraguay*, Asunción, 2006
Poulter, R., *Sabres across the Pampa. The Argentinian Indian Wars*, Partizan Press, 2012
Puliafito, C., *La Legione Italiana a Bahia Blanca, 1856*, Deipupi, 2011
Pulido Ramirez, G., *De Carabobo al Cerro de La Mona*, Editorial Amolca, 2014
Roca Maichel, L. E., *Historia de los Uniformes Militares de Colombia, 1810–1998*, Bogotá, 1998
Rodrigues, J. W., Barroso, G., *Uniformes do Exército Brasileiro, 1730–1922*, Rio de Janeiro, 1922
Rueda Cardozo, J. A., *Los ejércitos federales de Colombia 1855–1886*, Bucaramanga, 2013
Sanchez, L. F., *Soldados de Siempre*, La Paz, 2003
Sodré, N. W., *História militar do Brasil*, São Paulo, 1965
Thibaud, C., *Republicas en armas: Los ejércitos bolivarianos en la Guerra de Independencia en Colombia y Venezuela*, Editorial Planeta Colombiana, 2003
Udaondo, E., *Uniformes Militares usados en la Argentina desde el Siglo XVI hasta Nuestros Días*, Buenos Aires, 1922